HOW TO BEGIN WHEN
YOUR WORLD IS ENDING

Also by Molly Phinney Baskette

Remembering My Grandparent: A Kid's Own Grief Workbook in the Christian Tradition (with Nechama Liss-Levinson)

Remembering My Pet: A Kid's Own Spiritual Workbook for When a Pet Dies (with Nechama Liss-Levinson)

Real Good Church: How Our Church Came Back from the Dead and Yours Can, Too

Standing Naked Before God: The Art of Public Confession

Bless This Mess: A Modern Day Guide to Faith and Parenting in a Chaotic World (with Ellen O'Donnell)

HOW TO BEGIN

WHEN YOUR

WORLD

IS ENDING

A Spiritual Field Guide to Joy DESPITE Everything

MOLLY PHINNEY BASKETTE

Broadleaf Books

Minneapolis

HOW TO BEGIN WHEN YOUR WORLD IS ENDING
A Spiritual Field Guide to Joy Despite Everything

Cover design: Studio Gearbox

Print ISBN: 978-1-5064-8160-9
eBook ISBN: 978-1-5064-8161-6

This is a work of creative nonfiction. I have drawn material from my public blog, private journals, emails, and public testimonies by people in the churches I have served, as well as my own flawed and certainly subjective memory. Preachers, including me, often take poetic license for the sake of narrative flow. I also had new conversations with those whose stories I tell—parishioners, friends and family members—including sending them early drafts and allowing them to correct the record, change identifying details, choose pseudonyms, or create composite characters with my assistance.

I tell everything that happened from my own perspective and tried not to make myself the hero of this story, but that wily old ego will creep in. I hope you will sense both the full humanity and the tenderness I hold for every person in this book, just as they are, and as they (and I, and you) are all still becoming. We all contain multitudes.

To all the people, in all of my churches and throughout my life,
who have been God with skin on.

~

Jesus said, "You ought always to pray and not to faint."
Do not pray for easy lives;
      pray to be stronger people.
Do not pray for tasks equal to your powers,
      but for power equal to your tasks.
Then the doing of your work will be no miracle—
      you will be the miracle.
Every day you will wonder at yourself and at the richness of life
      which has come to you by the grace of God.

                                          —Julia Esquivel

CONTENTS

THERE ARE VERY FEW EMERGENCIES

If you are unlucky, or that is to say, an ordinary human, you have emergencies. The thing you found in your teenager's room. The lump you found in the shower. The phone call that changes everything.

When I first heard the shocking news that I had a ball of cancer growing sneakily and silently inside of me, the first call I made was to my husband. By tacit agreement, I'd been the unflappable one for the previous decade of our lives. But this time, he agreed to let me do most of the freaking out. It made that particular emergency a lot more bearable.

I first learned unflappability from a Robertson Davies novel, in which a village parson is called to the scene of a murder in the middle of the night. He doesn't race to the scene wild-haired with his PJs peeking out of his raincoat. He takes time to dress, wash, and compose himself before he gets there. He knows that whomever he meets at the other end will need his dignity, empathy, and strength—even if he would have to fake it in the face of the calamitous.

When I became a pastor, I took this role to heart, which doesn't mean I always get it right. There was the time I raced to the ER to support a mom fleeing partner violence in the middle of the night. My car had gotten broken into earlier that day, and there was still broken glass everywhere. The exhausted mother and her two kids had to wait in the dismal, cold 1 a.m. hospital parking lot while I sweatily cleaned off the seat before driving them to a hotel for the night.

Then there was the time I cried my eyes out in public on the church lawn after a particularly fierce church fight, my heart broken at news earlier that week that my only brother had died by violence. Broken afresh by the pettiness and awfulness of anxious church people facing big decisions and putting me in their crosshairs, I wept.

There was the time I, a newly minted mother, brought my newborn to a restorative justice circle between a confirmed pedophile and the parents of the child he had sexually assaulted. I couldn't line up childcare, and I thought I could manage it the way I'd handled so many other demanding, complex things in my life. (Whether it was the massive denial or just the cluelessness of being a new parent, I can't say.) My boy fussed, my boobs geysered ever-flowing streams, and I tried to low-key nurse with awkward beginning breastfeeding skills, holding back tears during one of the most devastating conversations I've ever participated in.

These are exceptions (I think. I expect some notes from people in the know.) Mostly, over the years, I've learned to pause when there are big feelings or big doings around me. I check in with God, who reminds me that whatever I'm about to face is not quite the emergency I imagine. And I take my cues from there.

That's what people in crisis need from God and God's customer service reps: those of us offering first-line spiritual support. Someone recently devastated by the unimaginable looks into our face as they would look into a mirror. What they hope to see is that they will get through this.

And they will. We have, all of us, so far survived everything we've been through, to one degree or another. We know because we are still here. As for those who didn't survive—those who have died, by their own hand or another's, by the villains of cancer or other catastrophes—my take is a question: do we really know they haven't survived, too? (More on that later.)

When I began writing this book, I was sheltering in place along with forty million other Californians as well as people in every other state and around the world. We were hiding out not from a mass shooter, or an alien invasion, but from a microscopic virus similar in design to the common cold that we were told could kill up to 3 percent of the global population. Maybe *this* qualified as an emergency?

Eight weeks into the shelter order, the biggest problem in our house was that my husband was rationing toilet paper. I told him he could decide how many squares per week I could have when he grew a vagina. Meanwhile, India, a country with one billion people, went into lockdown with only four hours' notice. Not enough time to purchase rice and beans, let alone toilet paper.

This pandemic changed all of our lives. It also ended many of our lives.

My biggest problem wasn't really the TP. Besides the expected anxieties about getting sick, my asthmatic children getting sick, or my elderly dad dying alone, I was sick at heart because I couldn't do my job the way I wanted to. Prudence and the internet dictated that, with my skill set, the most heroic thing I could do was stay home and binge-watch something called *Tiger King*.

I craved a larger purpose.

My arms ached from the hugs bottled up inside them. I wanted to get back to work helping people make meaning, if not sense, from the terrible things that happen to them, and I wanted to be able to do it in person, with a hand on their arm, and with a gaze directly into their eyes.

Because as much as I believe in God, and as much as I have felt the purely spiritual presence of God throughout my life, I need God to show up with skin on at regular intervals. We need a solid Someone who can help us feel the ground beneath our feet when fear or anxiety or anger are spinning out of control, a Someone to restore us to sanity, generosity, patience, and peace.

We need a Someone who teaches us how to do it for Someone Else, otherwise, we might die alone in our billionaire bunkers or MMA fighting in aisle three over the last container of disinfecting wipes.

I wanted to get back to work as this someone for others—because I've had so many Someones do it for me.

When I was young, everything felt like an emergency. My mother had incapacitating clinical depression and anxiety. My stepfather was a mentally ill alcoholic. My loving yet conflict-averse father followed my mother's whims about visitation and custody, hoping to stay on her good side, afraid of losing access to us entirely. I often felt like I was on my own, fending for myself.

I was on my own, but not alone. Angels accompanied me unawares. My Head Start teachers in preschool, the public librarian who let me read the second-grade books in first grade, my middle-school drama teacher, Mr. Casey—they all made safe new worlds for me to escape into when mine was too bleak. I took shelter in grades and achievement, a trusty launchpad to rocket me out of the poverty and chaos that often dogged my early life.

But even with angels beside me and a path before me, my emotions careened wildly. Until I turned twenty-eight, I pretty much cried nearly every day of my life. At twenty-eight, the river of tears finally slowed to a seasonal creek. The change came about because, in short, by then I had been loved well by enough Someones that I could become a Someone more frequently for others.

By my late twenties, I had found a series of best friends who are among the strongest people I've ever known. Their love enabled me to become my own solid self. Their love taught me how to be independent.

By that time, I had also made a casual friend, who became an ardent lover, and eventually a lifelong partner. Through many efficacious battles during the early years of our courtship and marriage, he helped me grow into a person who could sit tight through a fight—and learn to bend without breaking. He was the Someone who taught me how to be interdependent. And he was the Someone who I called with my lump news, who took on the Robertson Davies pastor role, so I could be among those who wail, bereft.

When I graduated from seminary, I wasn't sure I was ready to be a pastor because I knew people would have certain expectations of me and I didn't feel ready to bear that weight. I was worried about splitting into a public self who held it together and had all the answers and a private self who still fell apart on the regular. I needed to make sure my own self and stuff were managed so I wouldn't bleed out on people who needed me to meet them with focus and respect in their moment of need.

It was time to do unto others as so many Someones had done unto me. It was time to help them through the disasters in their lives, to remind them that the root word in emergency is *emerge.*

When I say that there are very few emergencies, I don't mean truly terrible things don't happen. I mean that if we can do things like breathe, delay gratification, feel our feelings in real time, keep ourselves from too much impulsivity, and reach for the right practice or people, we can survive—we can emerge—through disaster. If we can't make sense of what is happening to us and around us, we can at least make meaning, eventually.

And with spiritual hindsight, many of our disasters might turn out to be Holy Spirit portals: the way God gets in.

Sometimes, disaster creates a rupture with a reality that wasn't quite working. The woman who fled her home in the night is now in a new apartment, has a permanent restraining order, and is starting college alongside her eighteen-year-old son.

The pedophile did a five-year prison term, where he took advantage of every class and program and Bible study there to help him understand his affliction and gain empathy for his victims so that he would never re-offend. Later, he moved to a community with other sex offenders in recovery so he could have long-term support and accountability.

The boy who I nursed just left home to make his way through a country of virus, back to the place where he was born, to be birthed again into young adulthood.

My church and I are still emerging from our own emergency: a fire that claimed most of our church campus and drove us into deep disagreement and anxiety about our future. But recently, we all sent mail-in ballots to every member, asking them to approve the tearing up of part of our parking lot in order to build fifty units of affordable housing, one small but mighty effort to address the Bay Area housing crisis.

If the church had not burned down, we never would have taken this idea seriously. And we probably would not have brought it to a vote if coronavirus and sheltering-in-place had not revealed what really matters.

In the hardest way, we have learned that church is not a building, but a people—people who are called to be Someones for others.

And my husband held up his part of the bargain, to keep his shit together so I could fall all the way apart. I have had ten years of clean CT scans since that phone call to tell him the terrible news: no evidence of disease, even if lots of other evidence from the cancer and chemo remains after bombing my life ten years ago.

This is a book about the Someones I have pastored through some of the hardest things life can throw our way. It's a book about my own cancer odyssey and a tapestry of other stories about trying to face life on life's terms. Because some of us long to feel that "God is good, all the time," even if the world is definitely not.

It's a book for anyone who craves confirmation that even while God may not be the Great Puppet Master to make it all come right, Someone is present in our lives, loves us very much, and can provide strength and meaning.

It's a book for anyone who wants to press the bruise of the reality that this sweet, hard, wonderful gig of being human is going to come to an end someday, maybe sooner than we expect.

People training for the ministry inevitably take a seminary course called "Systematic Theology" about the nature and being of God, the concepts of sin, salvation, heaven, hell, grace, redemption, resurrection, prayer, and more. At progressive seminaries, we see all of these through the lenses of structural racism and sexism, colonialism and liberation theology. As at an eye exam, when the optometrist flips the lens, we say, "Now we see more clearly. Yes, more clearly now."

The goal of the course is to arrange the religious truths we are learning into a self-consistent whole, without gaps, helping us better teach and pastor the people in our care during times of crisis or struggle. In a classroom setting, it is a blueprint for a boat of sorts. But we don't yet know if the blueprint will create a seaworthy vessel. The only way to know is to test the boat in real-world conditions, out on the open sea.

This book is about testing the seaworthiness of the vessel. The blueprints came from the class, but God and I built this ship together and tested it through some of the very hardest things that can happen to humans. As a parish minister, I encounter people at their most vulnerable, aching, confused, and frail. I have pastored people convicted of rape and murder, those living with treatment-resistant depression, PTSD, unremitting eating disorders, domestic and sexual abuse survivors, those suffering through pregnancy loss and the death of a child, divorce, or those fleeing violence in another country, and those coming out as queer to fundamentalist parents or discerning their true gender.

Every one of those experiences tested seaworthiness. Every one made that boat, and God, more real. Every one of those experiences forced me to throw overboard the things that threatened to sink us, and showed me where to find a lifebuoy I could throw to save life, give hope, banish fear, and help someone find their way back from despair or toward redemption.

———

Life as it stands will keep trying to shake us up or smash our boat onto the rocks. This is not because God is an asshole. It's because Nature throws novel viruses and earthquakes and worse into our path. It's also because humans are inventive and wonderful, but then we dream up things that ruin lives, like crystal meth, hypercapitalism, and high-waisted jeans (not a good look for anyone).

If we think we are safe, we are wrong. Nothing can insulate us from loss. But safe was never the point. There are fates worse than death—like not ever really living.

If you are lucky, you are currently between emergencies. Maybe you've had a rare chance to get off the roller coaster entirely. Your legs have just stopped shaking, and you think, "I'm never doing *that* again." You are sitting in the sun, eating something delicious and terrible for you: fried dough, a corn dog, a caramel apple that will pull out your crown. Enjoy the moment. It's not going to last.

And if you are in the middle of a fast-moving or slow-motion emergency—a sick toddler, a wayward teen, a relationship at a crossroads, a dance with addiction, a mental health crisis—only time will tell if it really was a true emergency. Because with the right kind of attention, ruptures can reveal us, emerge us, and help us evolve faster than any virus.

By the time you are reading this, we are (hopefully!) past the worst of the global pandemic. You, like God, are living in the future and have divine hindsight. You have grieved your dead, and your grief, with any grace, has softened into blessed memory. Maybe the pandemic will have proven to be a portal to universal paid sick leave, universal basic income, universal health care, and universal Earth care. Millions may have died, but they will not have died in vain.

Because God is not an asshole. And while God didn't send the disaster, God for damn sure will use it.

Chapter 1

GOD DIDN'T SEND THE DISASTER (BUT SHE WILL USE IT)

Every day, your body makes new cells. Epithelial cells, dendritic cells, neutrophils, platelets, and two hundred other varieties. And every day, when your body is making new cells, one of them, often more than one, goofs up in dividing. That cell turns into a cancer cell. It's a trash cell, serving no purpose beyond making more and more and more of itself—a natural narcissist. Lucky for you, your body then sends a white blood cell known as a natural killer cell to take out the trash.

Until the day when your body misses one.

Every day, things in life go wrong and then suddenly go right again, often without our even noticing. But sometimes things go wrong, and keep going wrong.

When bad things happen to us, our reptilian brains seek the shelter of easy answers and black-and-white thinking and look for a culprit: God! Often the first, most convenient target. In January 2010, a 7.0 earthquake struck Haiti, the poorest country in the Western Hemisphere, killing 250,000 people and displacing another 1.5 million. The city I lived in at the time, Somerville, Massachusetts, has a sizable Haitian population. A prayer vigil was arranged in the high-school gym, and I was invited to pray.

As I waited my turn, I listened to pastor after pastor lament that God was punishing Haiti for some sin they had committed. They weren't even blaming God. They were blaming *themselves*. It's what victims sometimes do, if only to take back some control over the narrative of chaos. (Not to mention, it is what a racist, sexist, classist, and homophobic society has taught them to do.) You shouldn't have been jogging in that neighborhood. You asked for it by wearing that skirt. You must be lazy or stupid if you can't get ahead in America.

Not today, Satan. Throwing out my notes, I asked the Holy Spirit for a new prayer.

"Holy One, I know You didn't send this disaster. But I know You want to use it. Haiti has been the poorest country in the Western Hemisphere since its people became the first to win freedom from their enslavers and the rest of the world abandoned it. God, richer countries have turned a blind eye to Haiti's suffering time and time again. But we can't look away now. Use this earthquake to break the hard hearts of the many of us who have forgotten that Haiti is our neighbor."

Three months after I prayed that prayer, I was suddenly diagnosed with cancer. They found the tumor in my left lung of all places. An errant golf ball lodged there inside my rib cage for who knows how long, as I breathed in, breathed out, oblivious to the ticking time bomb.

It was a chance to test the earthquake prayer under very personal circumstances: the idea that God didn't send the disaster, but She would use it.

She would take advantage of the rupture and the pain—great stimulants—to make all kinds of things happen that might not have otherwise. And not just to change and reveal me to myself in essential ways but also to shape the many lives that touched mine. Because God is like that: doing more than one thing at the same time.

Obviously, I lived. And, spoiler alert: cancer radically reoriented me toward life, even saved my life, in ways I will never completely be able to understand.

I can say this *because* I got to live. I'm writing this from the future. I might have quite different things to say about cancer if it had killed me, cut short my marriage and my calling, and orphaned my children.

Not that everything turned out all right in the end. Life goes on, in equilibrium and disequilibrium. Good things happen, thorny problems resolve, and then, if you are lucky, you live long enough for life to get hard again. Since surviving cancer, I have also survived my brother's murder, suicide attempts by two people I helped raise, my now fifteen-year-old's clinical depression, and the ongoing roller coaster of my nineteen-year-old's flirtations with things that might kill him (if we don't do it first). Also, a cross-country move, a major fire, and a Donald Trump presidency (fist-bump).

When new members join my church, they go through an initiation. We invite them to a house in the Berkeley Hills for a festive evening of crepes, sparkling beverages, and spiritual stories as the sun sets over the Bay. The experience of telling a circle of random strangers who to outward appearances have nothing in common how God has shown up in their life (or left them hanging) strips them bare. There are always tears, sometimes deep sobbing, shared grief, furious nodding, along with lots of laughter and gallows humor. We leave knowing we have shared a foxhole for a few hours.

Before the stories are told and as we sit down with full plates teetering on our laps, I tell them, "Your faith story is not your church story. It is much bigger than that, and might only be a little bit about church. It also is probably not a sweet, easy story."

I guide them through the process and offer ideas. "To figure out how to tell it, you might use geographic motifs like the Bible does: a mountaintop experience, the valley of the shadow of death, the valley of dry bones, a great flood, wandering in the desert, a shipwreck, the getting-eaten-then-barfed-up by a great beast, or the testing time alone in the wilderness with only angels and demons for company.

"Your story might be relational: about makeups, breakups, significant mentors, deaths, and other losses.

"Your story might be an incarnational story of bodily illness, recovery, wounds, scars, and resurrection."

Every story is unique, but through years of listening to stories told in faith and vulnerability, I see common themes. One particular tale comes up again and again: as a precocious seven-year-old in Sunday school, thirteen-year-old in confirmation class, or nineteen-year-old in Bible college, they started asking their teachers uncomfortable theological questions.

Questions like, "How could a good God condemn people to eternal suffering in hell?" "What do you do about all the contradictions in the Bible or the scriptural rules we conveniently ignore?" "What would Jesus have to say about how institutional Christianity has made racism, sexism, homophobia, transphobia, xenophobia, and a weird, creepy, 'America-first' patriotism part of its operating system?"

And while we're on the subject, if God is really in charge of all of this, how come children die hungry or get sex trafficked? How is it possible that a man who cheats on, abandons, or kills his wife can be redeemed by God, but a woman who leaves her abusive marriage can't take communion? And how dare God wipe out hundreds of thousands of people with a single tsunami, earthquake, or plague?

With few exceptions, our new members tell us how they began to critique the party line. How they move from what the theologian Marcus Borg called *precritical naïveté* into a more mature critical thinking posture. The stories include how their teachers, bent on keeping control, couldn't handle the questions and usually kicked them out.

After that, one of a few things happened to them. Sometimes, they surveyed their other options and found a more progressive Christian church where they could ask all the questions, and have all the feelings, and nobody would raise an eyebrow.

Often, they found their way down new spiritual paths that didn't leave such a bad taste in their mouths: Buddhism, Hinduism, or Judaism, where they could read a lot of the same sacred texts without the Christian supersessionism and fundamentalist malpractice.

Most often, they gave up religion as a bad deal, shook the dust off their sandals, and left the church entirely, becoming functional agnostics or atheists. Sunday morning turned into a haven for jammies and the comics section or vigorous communion with God through nature and high-tech athleisure wear.

But some were too stubborn to leave their conservative churches. They refused to go quietly, but they also refused to submit to teachings that made no logical or moral sense. So they stayed, and some of them made their own sense out of what they were hearing.

Like Ashley, a young mom who recently joined our church. She was raised in Oklahoma by a scientist dad and a religious mom whose faith compelled the whole family to church. As a teen, Ashley started going to her friend's more evangelical church because they had better snacks, cute boys, and a really charismatic youth pastor who played guitar. Her new church provided the comfort of ritual and belonging and a strong container that defined and made sense of the world through the terrifying, disorienting teen years.

But as Ashley learned in ever greater detail just who was welcomed into the country club of God's grace and approval—and who was consigned to hell based on the most arbitrary criteria—she said, "I decided that if God was going to do that to so many of the people I loved, then God was real, but an asshole."

"God is an asshole" is a legitimate bus stop on the faith journey. It's a place to set down our baggage for a while and rest. But it's not the destination.

The stories that get told amongst our new members reveal that the faith journey is not a straight road, but a spiral. We don't move up a gentle slope at a consistent pace toward a God with open arms. We find God, we lose God, or we feel that God has lost us. We spiral back to the same obsessions, fears, addictions, and quandaries. We temporarily take refuge in our own strong containers and fundamentalisms, some of which leave a lot of people out (and we discover that progressives can also be fundamentalists).

Yesterday, we didn't believe that God was all-powerful or that God meted out cancer or catastrophes to an unlucky few. But today, after talking to the doctor, we wail to God, "Why MEEEE?" It's primal thinking: Humans have blamed God for disasters since Jesus died on the cross, since Noah started gathering wood for the ark, since we began to scratch paintings of tsunamis on cave walls, since … we were human. We have always looked for a scape-goat to blame when traumatic times come upon us.

The disaster is not a lightning bolt from the hand of God. It is sometimes the fruit of our free will, the hard use of humans by one another. It is some-times Earth's organic yawing, pitching, gravity run amok, Nature being red in tooth and claw. Disaster is not personal. It is the price we pay for being alive on this particular planet.

Most of us will not get through life unscathed. Resiliency comes not just from suffering but the type of suffering that finds a broader perspective and the right supports to help us decide what to do next.

This is easy to say from my white, middle-class perch. I may have had my own early challenges, but my color, my education, and my other privileges have made it easier for me. At the same time, people from similar circumstances—even siblings in the same family—respond very differently under duress.

When Cathie was 5 years old, she completely stopped talking as a result of the physical, emotional, and sexual abuse she suffered in her adoptive home. She says God blessed her with mutism, a way of protecting herself from what was happening to her at a very powerless time. The mutism came and went through her teen years, and at age 20, emancipated from her family, she walked into a neighborhood mental health clinic, speechless once more.

When the first available therapist came out, she quickly recognized that Cathie was unable to speak. She proceeded to talk to her gently in a one-sided conversation, at the end of which she said, "You only need to answer one ques-tion. Will you come back next week at this same time?" Cathie answered yes.

"What followed was a wonderful emotional and psychological separation between my mother and myself. After growing up believing that I was the cause of everything bad that happened in my life, I began to understand that God had been with me all the time and loved me very, very much. That my mother was responsible for her own actions and I could begin to live a separate life from her if I chose to.

"That was the big question. Did I now choose to take responsibility for my own life with God's love and constant grace, and continue to get the help I needed in order to get mentally healthy?

"The answer was a positive and life affirming YES! God, from a very early age in my life, became my best friend, and remains my best friend to this day."

Cathie had a series of therapists from then on, some more helpful, some less, until she came out of a hospitalization at age fifty and found a new counselor, Nancy. Nancy's warm and expansive mother-love was just what Cathie needed. But Nancy also made her work hard through the early trauma that had dogged her entire life. "There were times when I was so exhausted from the work that she would read me children's books at the end of our sessions!" But the effort paid off—it allowed her to love herself more fully than she ever had, and in doing so, begin to forgive those who had failed her, and become a healthier mother to her now-adult daughter. But Cathie didn't stop there. She turned her own healing into healing for others.

Professionally, she chose to work in special education until she was sixty-two, and then as an in-home care provider until she was seventy. She once offered this testimony in church:

"My whole adult career has been carefully chosen because of how I spent my childhood. Working with children with special needs, and adults who need love and care in their senior years, has filled my heart with joy! In so many ways, it has helped heal some very deep wounds. My heart is full of gratitude for the many people that have been and continue to be my allies. As a child, I was alone, but as an adult, God has given me a village. Thank you so much loving God!"

Cathie moved away from Berkeley a couple of years ago to be closer to her daughter and grandchildren. But she still participates in every online activity of our church and has recently become a leader of our mental health ministry. Even from afar, she is blessing us, and being part of the village she needed to heal.

I could tell dozens of these stories from among the saints I have served in my churches. Stories of religious abuse so severe it left the victim unable to hear the mostly reliably comforting scripture quotes or hymns without flashbacks because of how those chestnuts had been "interpreted" by the perpetrator. Stories of siblings sitting well-behaved in the front pew on Sunday morning next to their parents, only to go home to be violently abused by older siblings Sunday night while their parents turned a blind eye. Stories of people manipulated and violated by their pastors or youth leaders when they were at their most vulnerable.

And still, these beloveds haven't given up on God or even church. Betrayed and abandoned by their churches or "religious" family members, brainwashed using Biblical language and symbols, nonetheless they keep showing up for their own healing and transcendence, to claim their rightful place in religious community, to be a people for others, and to stand as examples of God deeply at work in and on them.

Every one of us gets an invitation to resurrection. It comes in a little ivory envelope, delivered directly to our souls, right after the disaster happens. Sometimes, we miss it. Sometimes, we open it much later. Sometimes, we tear it open with eager hands. You don't have to be an optimist to accept this invitation. But you do have to be curious about what will happen next, if it will be different from the pain of right now, and if *you* will be different. Curiosity and longing will take you pretty far in life, no matter how bad things are in the moment.

Rebecca Solnit's beautiful book *A Paradise Built in Hell* tells stories from four different epic disasters, like the 1906 San Francisco earthquake and Hurricane Katrina. She describes what she calls "disaster utopia": how disasters can bring out the best in us by calling on our spontaneous, generous, communitarian impulses; the fierce, structural mother-energy that lives in us all, dormant, just waiting for the right moment; and a soaring sense of purpose. "Horrible in itself," she writes, "disaster is sometimes a door back into paradise, the paradise at least in which we are who we hope to be, do the work we desire, and are each other's keepers."

God is always doing more than one thing at the same time.

Disaster is a force that lays us bare, that reveals deep social and societal truths, that makes us face ourselves and our systems in a way that invites us to change. *Apocalypse*, a different word for disaster that is seasoned with mysticism, literally means "revealing."

Some traditions say Jesus went to hell after he died in order to empty it and bring everyone to heaven. His death exposed the inherent violence of the system. It was intended, like the civil rights movement's strategy of non-violence, to expose hatred and violence to sanitizing sunlight and alchemize them into love.

Whether or not you believe in a literal resurrection, imagine that every time love defeats fear, anger, or violence, Jesus comes alive again. Every day, somewhere, resurrection is happening. It has happened to me at least seventeen times. Still, resurrection does require a death.

"We devote much of our lives to achieving certainty, safety and comfort," writes Rebecca Solnit, "but with them often comes ennui and a sense of meaninglessness; the meaning is in the struggle, or can be, and one of the complex questions for those who need not struggle for basic survival is how to engage passionately with goals and needs that keep such drive alive—the search for meaning that Viktor Frankl wrote about after Auschwitz."

When I was child, I suffered and even dodged death more than once. As a four-year-old froggering across multiple big city streets to buy cigarettes for my mother, too flattened by depression to go herself. As an eight-year-old cling-riding behind my drunk stepfather on his motorcycle through snowy streets.

The teen years weren't any easier. Life was deeply distressing at sixteen for a thousand different reasons: my B-minus in gym, the boy who waxed hot and cold, the social mafia who orchestrated my public shaming by way of yearbook superlatives—not to mention we were going on year seven of a Reagan presidency. It was all just too much. But I couldn't really muster the necessary energy to kill myself. It seemed like an awful lot of work. Also, it would be a permanent solution to what might turn out to be a temporary set of problems.

Decades passed. I scrabbled through heartaches and setbacks and marginal successes, and adventures in adulting, and by the time I reached thirty-nine, life was pretty good. I had a loving husband, Peter, who was usually my best friend. Amid the pain of several miscarriages, we were finally parents to a three-year-old daughter, Carmen, and a seven-year-old son, Rafe. I had a stable, rewarding, and demanding job as the pastor of a small but growing church. I had a 401k and a Toyota Echo we had bought new, even if it smelled mysteriously of cheese most of the time (see afore-mentioned kids).

And I found myself coming into some of the ennui that Solnit describes. I had survived—but for what? While I had a good-enough marriage and was a good-enough mother, some patterns desperately needed breaking. First among them, the long-standing capoeira battle with my delightful and exasperating firstborn, who brought out the worst in me: perfectionism, imperiousness, and fury.

I had been a workaholic most of my life since deciding at age eleven that workaholism was the opposite of my family's addictions instead of my own substitute. I had built a stronger ego for myself out of achievement, but still felt pursued by a monster that threatened to undo me. Every time I stopped or slowed the pace, I feared again that poverty or congenital mental illness would eat me alive.

Changing patterns is a key that unlocks spiritual growth. My spiritual director and I decided maybe the world wouldn't stop and my church crash and burn if I stopped working so hard. I took a sabbatical, and my family and I spent the summer in lavender and Meyer lemon–scented Northern California.

But when we went home to Boston, I slipped right back into the workaholic groove. Within weeks, I developed a herniated disk in my lower back. It was excruciating. Some days it was so bad my husband would have to tie my shoes while I wept in pain and fear. Sometimes, I asked him to bite my arm to distract me from the agony in my back. When we have silenced our souls, our bodies have a way of talking to us.

In the journal entries of those days, an odd little omen showed what awaited me in the next chapter of my medical journey:

October 18, 2009

I went to bed last night, feeling the good weight of routine and happy monotony on my shoulders, wondering with the minority opinion part of myself, "Is this all there is? Wake up achy and creaky, work it out through the morning, zoom through the day with kids/work/kids/work, make dinner, glassawine, rush through bedtime so I can have 'me' time to watch an episode or two of *Scrubs*?"

Then the majority opinion part of myself said, "Yes, this is all there is, for this moment, and what's wrong with that? What's wrong with being constrained from hitchhiking through Europe or writing a terrible novel because you have an incredibly interesting and challenging job, and two children who make you laugh and hug all day long, and a husband who (most of the time) is funny, kind and warm? Does Zach Braff cover your face with kisses, refuse to release you, and say 'Mom, one Last Important Kiss, okay?'"

Taking stock, last night, was because I got called to Mass General yesterday to visit [my parishioner Jeff's mom] Pat. She's not a lapsed Catholic so much as a furious one, who still goes to mass, but gets in the face of the priests when their homilies take them off the rails of real life. She has pancreatic cancer, and told me, in private, that she wants to have her funeral at our church whenever her time comes. Fucking cancer. One day, she's walking around fine. The next day, her primary care doctor is saying things to her like, "Three percent survival rate."

But, Peter says, "She's sixty, and she didn't take good care of herself."

But, I remind him that Christopher, our totally healthy Christian Buddhist friend, died of brain cancer two years ago at age thirty-eight, leaving two babies behind.

"But," he said, "flukes."

"But," I said, "it sure makes me enjoy my monotony."

November 3, 2009

I wept openly at spiritual direction today. For the first time. I realized how old my frail, creaky body in pain all the damn time is making me feel.

"How is your soul doing?" my director said. "It feels young!" I said. *And deeply at odds with my body*, I thought. Probably this is just my quiet, well-hidden, pessimistic, and superstitious self, the shadow of the faith-face I show the world, but I feel like I'm getting ready for death. Everything within me rises up and says "Wait, wait! I want to know my children as adults. I want to meet my grandchildren!" Last night, Carmen, age three, and I were joking about her being a chick and growing up to be a hen. "And when my babies pop out," she said, "they will be chicks! Will you help me take care of them?"

I'm not giving these fears much airtime, mostly because I got literally eighty emails yesterday and have to plow through them before attempting (ouch) to work out in spite of my killer pain, meeting with a dissatisfied member of the church to do an exit interview, and picking up the kids early so I can get to the MRI for my pelvis and back...but it is consuming me, I realize.

Strangely, I feel close to God, and have been praying a lot, but have not prayed once about this—the pain, the aging, and wanting it all to go away, to move through me and past me.

December 26, 2009

I've been praying to God for like a month now to take the pain away, take it away. I cried about it to my spiritual director again and he asked me if the pain made me shake my fist at God and ask, "Why????"

I said no. I feel more like a little kid with cancer in a hospital bed, staring up at my parent with pleading eyes, confused.

I was swimming after spiritual direction the other day and our conversation had opened some things up in my mind. *Why, why?* I finally did start asking. *Why this, now?* I thought of the Rumi poem "Jesus on the Lean Donkey," the man who'd accidentally swallowed a poisonous serpent, the God-figure throwing apples at him and shouting at him to eat so he would vomit up the serpent and live. I thought of God hobbling us, permitting only certain things, so we have to travel a narrow path.

The pain was constant, and often unbearable, but I was raised by my hippie father, George, to believe that vitamin C and apple cider vinegar (and the occasional joint) were the cure for almost everything, so I refused surgery for six months. I finally caved.

Strangely, I both looked forward to surgery and its hinted promise of relief and felt guilty about it. It felt like failure. I was still laboring under the mindset I was supposed to heal myself with positive thinking, prayer, nutrition, and stinky Chinese herbs.

I found myself wishing I could take the advice I gave everybody else: God sends healing in many forms, and it is blasphemy to say that God will give it only through, say, laying hands, and not through proven surgical technique.

Dr. Friedberg, the neurosurgeon, was no hand-holder. He told me that with back surgery there were no guarantees, but he could do some basic carpentry on my spine. He had pretty good outcomes and he thought I was a reasonable candidate.

Then this science-minded, dispassionate surgeon said the most astonishingly woo-woo thing. "It's really your decision," he said. "It's about your quality of life. Sometimes, there are other reasons we can't see, other factors at stake. Last year, one of my patients decided to get the surgery after all, and when we did his presurgical testing, the blood work turned up leukemia."

"Uh, thanks, Doc," I said. "This is supposed to reassure me?"

"Well, we caught it. And he's doing okay now."

I booked surgery for the Tuesday after Easter 2010. Holy Week is the week leading up to Easter and the marathon for parish ministers, with eight or nine very different worship services in as many or fewer days. I decided to go for presurgical testing before Palm Sunday to get it out of the way before our Sweeps Week began.

Then, the night before testing, I had a dream. A dream that was no dream at all, but God coming to me from the future.

Chapter 2

HOW TO MYSTICAL

When I was fifteen, I wanted to be a witch. What I *really* wanted to be was more powerful than I felt as a gangly, socially awkward teen, and to have my crush bestow on me a perfect first French kiss. But how those desires manifested was me frequenting a magic store called Arsenic and Old Lace in North Cambridge, and spending all my babysitting money on love potions and books about candle spells.

My first serious foray into the magical and mystical (aside from childhood, when we are *all* witches by nature) was in seventh grade. My girlfriends and I had an enormous collective crush on Duran Duran that risked cascading into stalkerdom. We had somehow seized the idea of astral projection as a way of bridging the obvious social and geographic gulfs between us and the British pop superstars we were obviously intended for. We would just have to learn how to leave our bodies, and our insistent hearts would fly us directly to Simon Le Bon and John Taylor, wherever they were, probably writing the hit follow-up to "Union of the Snake" in some dim basement while chain-smoking Dunhills. What a cinch!

Jenny Kazarian, over the course of multiple sleepovers, convinced the rest of us that she'd done it. She'd astral projected! She regaled us with stories of jam seshes and make out extravaganzas so detailed and confident that we believed every word. Plus, if Jenny could do it, the rest of us couldn't be far behind. Night after night, in my little twin bed, I tried to will myself to leave my body, and for all my labored efforts, just got a crushing pain behind my left eyeball. My soul remained stubbornly attached to my corporeal form.

These early failures notwithstanding, my desire to touch other worlds, to plant myself in thin places, to access magic, never left me. It's at least part of the reason I became a minister. (No one will give you a salary and benefits to be a witch.)

Most of us long to pull ourselves out of the muck of the everyday, the sink full of dishes, the paperwork piling up on the desk. Whether as *Bewitched's* Samantha turning everything right with a twitch of her nose, or Galadriel, beautiful and terrible and bent on keeping the forces of evil at bay throughout Middle Earth, we want to influence the world for good and avoid the endless march toward entropy and lost socks.

And once in a while, we manage to do it. We have a mystical experience. We reach out a hand and feel we can push right through to another dimension. We know, wordlessly, that there is a deeper reality, that Someone is, if not strictly in *control*, at least in some kind of possession of these worlds. We can rest.

Mystical experiences, in and of themselves, are no measure of faithful living. I have pastored people who have come to church agog after having an intense and very mystical experience only to have them ghost again after its memory faded away. William came to our church after one such experience, his face set to permanent wonder (or maybe that was always his resting face). He had never been to church in his life but took to it like a native, never missing a Bible study, working the room at coffee hour.

But in time, he began showing up less and less, and eventually stopped returning my phone calls. One day, I ran into him in town, and because I am that person, I said, "What's up? We miss seeing you." He looked off into the distance and said something like, "I don't know. I guess I'm just not feeling it anymore."

I have also pastored people who have painfully longed to sense God's presence, only to be met with silence despite lifelong striving and serving. Liz did every thankless job in the early days of our struggling church. But her cries to God echoed back unanswered. Silence answered her even when she was deep-grieving her own miscarriage, and three years later, when the healthy newborn she had finally birthed suddenly fell sick with a respiratory virus and had to be hospitalized. Was Liz somehow not worthy of a message from God?

Then again, who's to say that God didn't lead William away from our church just as deftly as She did toward us? Maybe William was only "ours" for a season. God can turn down the volume on our spiritual soundtrack as surely as God can turn it up, and She has Her reasons.

And who's to say that even though Liz can't strictly perceive God's presence in her life, that God is not there? Just as some people have a finer sense of smell, are supertasters, or have perfect vision, while others have diminished senses. A few years after her newborn came through RSV with flying colors, Liz was hiking through the woods with her husband and two children. Out of nowhere, an enormous tree came down onto her four-year-old, who might have died, but was carried out of the woods alive with her arm broken in three places.

This is not to say, of course, that God loves and protects some people's newborns and four-year-olds while letting others suffer or die. I'll say more about why I believe God is not an asshole in regard to who lives and dies. But in case you are the kind of person who can't feel God palpably, I wanted to tell you about Liz. It doesn't mean you are not trying hard enough. It doesn't mean there is something broken or bad in you if God doesn't communicate with you directly.

I don't do candle spells anymore, but I still believe in all the magic. As my husband once said: once you decide to believe in God, you have to admit that anything is possible. Extraterrestrials. Faith healing. Ghosts.

Oddly, even though I'm cautiously open to all things mystical, it turns out I'm also a realist who gets shocked pretty much every time God makes Herself noisily known. I am a material girl, in a material world, and probably entirely too focused on the dress sale at Boden during my waking hours for God to get through to me on weekdays. God's dramatic entrances have happened often enough in my life that you would think I would start to expect them. But every time God talks directly to me, either with words written on my heart or a clear-as-a-bell voice that is wiser than mine, I admit it still feels like a shocking gift.

Once the voice spoke as I walked alone, terrified, down a rural road in the dark, without a flashlight. I had just graduated from college and was on a conveyor belt to a lifetime career with the State Department. I was increasingly certain the job would make me miserable, but it seemed to impress everybody else. Before heading to my job in DC, I had granted myself one last joyful pitstop on the dreadful road to adulthood, working at my happy place: a hippie Christian summer camp that had saved my life time and again through my teenage years.

This particular summer, I was working as Camp Family Mom to a group of teenagers who cleaned toilets for pennies an hour, and we all loved every minute of it. Our crew lived in a rustic cabin that could have been pinched from the set of a horror movie, a half-mile down a steep and windy hill from the rest of the staff.

I made it most of the way through the summer without getting stranded at bedtime, but one night accidentally, horribly found myself the last down-the-hill person still up the hill. On the moonless night, I set out at a run to the grim task of facing unseen werewolves or highway robbers. Except that I ran off the road into the even darker dark of the woods, having to feel my way, inch by inch, back toward the pavement. Blood clanged in my ears as I wondered if at the tender age of twenty-two I could die of fright.

That was when God said to me as clear as day, "I've been trying to get you alone." These are not really the words you want to hear from God, even if you feel God is more Kindly Presence than Skeezy Pickup Artist, or worse, Malevolent Jokester. But that's often how you know it *is* God, that surprise voice in the quiet.

God's voice is both kinder and sterner than I imagined. Then and now. It often tells me things I don't want to hear. He urges me onto a hard path that leads to far greater joy in living. My version of God may sound more like a stalker than a Hallmark card, but how often does a Hallmark card fix your life? Of course, God is as likely to ruin your life as fix it—though She will usually ruin it for the better.

That night, God didn't tell me I was supposed to send the State Department a Dear John letter and race off to seminary. That took a few more summer conversations, most of them with actual humans (God with skin on). It involved tears and misery, and a sad phone call to my disappointed agnostic father, who had tolerated my dabblings with religion, never expecting it to become a career.

But it was God who started the conversation there in the dark, getting me to slow my pace and feel my way forward, trusting the road beneath my feet even though the way was completely blocked from my sight.

I looked for opportunities to walk down the hill by myself at bedtime from then on, hoping to hear from God again. I didn't, not for a while. God is not a trained dog who will come at our calling. But there are circumstances in which we are much more likely to hear from God, usually involving loneliness and terror.

Another time I heard God loud and clear was when I was pregnant with our second child. After two miscarriages, I was about nine weeks along, the same point at which my previous pregnancies had ended and so sick at the thought of loss that I couldn't feel anything but fear. I'd hold my stomach all day long, freaking out at every twinge of my pelvic floor, trying as hard to will this pregnancy to stay in my body as I had, in seventh grade, willed my spirit to leave it.

I couldn't find words to pray for what I really wanted. Instead, for some reason, I just repeated over and over the Jesus prayer that I dimly remembered from Salinger's *Franny and Zooey*: "Lord Jesus Christ, Son of God, have mercy on me, a sinner." That prayer wasn't even my kind of religious language. I mean sure, I was a part-time sinner, like everyone, but I didn't believe that the miscarriages were a punishment from God. Nor, as much as I love Jesus, do I normally appeal to him in my prayers. I go straight to upper management. But the rhythmic quality of the prayer soothed me. It became a mantra, an end run around my activated lizard brain, something I could say when I couldn't find the words to get my heart's desire through the hot ball that jammed my throat.

I was praying this prayer one day as I drove to the hospital for an OB appointment that would give some indication of the pregnancy's viability. Suddenly, on the corner of Mt. Auburn and Channing Streets, God interrupted my prayer. "Do you want to know?"

Only if it's good news. I thought I said that bit to myself, but God overheard. I felt Their respectful pause, waiting for an answer.

"Please give me a healthy, full-term baby."

A glint entered God's voice. "I will give you something even better than that! Just wait and see."

"No, that'll do," I rushed in to say, "thanks, just like I asked, please. No more, no lesssssss!!!" but God was already done with the conversation and moved on.

About seven months later, in a splendid Broadway opening act that involved a cascade of medical maladies, including a torn uterus and an emergency C-section, our daughter, Carmen, arrived into our lives. She was seven pounds, four ounces of perfect, once they warmed her up from blue to pink.

I remembered God's strange promise, the blessing-curse that seemed like something from a shady fairy godmother à la Grimm. I kept quiet, hoping to stay under the radar. But it turns out the fairy-tale curse was just delayed in manifesting.

Five months later, the first time we fed Carmen something other than breast milk, we ended up at the hospital with a baby covered in welts and vomit. We discovered she had a host of life-threatening food allergies. Life with, and for, Carmen has been overshadowed by EpiPens, anaphylaxis, ER visits, and constant vigilance around food. When she grew into a six-year-old who could finally understand the "life-threatening" part of the phrase "life-threatening food allergies," she developed an imaginary enemy named Throwup who wanted her dead. That was the year we found her a great therapist.

When you face your own mortality every time you put a morsel of food in your mouth, it makes you very grateful to be alive. Carmen is deeply tuned in to God and is a girl who for her whole life has experienced full-scale "Golden God Moments" and the lesser mystical "warm tickles" as everyday events.

And having a difference that forced her to bring soy/peanut/tree nut/dairy-free cupcakes to kindergarten birthday parties at Chuck E. Cheese made her aware of other kinds of difference, difficulty, and disability. Even though in adolescence Carmen is becoming slowly liberated from most of her allergies, she remains an extremely compassionate kid, always on the lookout for the ones who are bullied, left out, or lonely. She understands her disability as a strength. The godmother curse turned out to be a blessing after all. Even Carmen will tell you that—well, most days.

But the most terrifying and real life-altering time I encountered God was the night before they found my tumor entirely by accident. I had a dream that was really a near-death experience masquerading as a dream, a dream in which I found out what happens when this life ends. I don't expect you to believe it. I scarcely believe it, even though it happened to me. It was the night before a scheduled routine test before back surgery, before any hint of cancer had breached the horizon.

I hate books like *Proof of Heaven* (discredited) and *Heaven Is for Real* (inconsistent); stories that want to manipulate and convince us that God is Real and we are all going to the pie in the sky someday.

I don't believe in a Santa-Claus God, delivering good things on cue. I do believe in a God who lures us from danger and toward the good, a gamifying God who leaves puzzle clues and Easter eggs everywhere. I believe in a God trying to communicate with us by any means possible. And how God often does this, at least to the doofy and distracted protagonists of the Bible stubbornly resistant to getting the message, is through dreams, where God shows them the future and gives them a choice.

In Genesis, Jacob took a journey home after a long absence and wrestled all night with an angel while en route. The next day, he reunited with the estranged brother he expected would want to murder him. Instead, he was met with an embrace. Then there's Joseph of the technicolor dream coat who saved the people of Egypt, his kin, and himself by interpreting the Pharaoh's dreams. And Joseph, the adoptive father of Jesus, was warned in a dream to take the newborn and Mary and spirit them to Egypt, away from murderous Herod, so Jesus could survive to do all that he did. In sacred dreams, life often gets yanked from the jaws of death.

I awoke from my own once-in-a-lifetime dream, a dream so radiantly real I did something I never do: I got up and wrote the whole thing down, despite the busy day ahead. When I later read the account, it illuminated everything without the suggestiveness of hindsight.

I was in a storefront church in a strip mall, surrounded by a group of young Latinx Christians. Some of them were real people I knew, children from the orphanage where my husband Peter and I had lived and worked a dozen years earlier, now grown into young adults. It was a Pentecostal church, and I was there as their guest.

They began to invite each other, one at a time, to step onto a dais to receive the Holy Spirit. I am normally plagued by the skeptical, cerebral posture of a mainline Protestant when I'm among more charismatic Christians. Maybe it's fear of being emotionally manipulated. Maybe it's the terror of actually having something supernatural happen. But this time, I wanted to take my turn on the dais: to have all my careful ego-boundaries and preconceptions and prejudices and fears suspended. I wanted to be struck by the Holy Spirit, come what may.

And I was. I stepped into the space and a woman named Damaris, whom I didn't recognize but for whom I felt an overpowering trust, looked at me with love and affection. She moved behind me and laid hands on me—and everything changed in an instant. I felt, then saw, my body slump to the floor. My spirit floated up, looking around, swimming, suspended, near the ceiling.

I felt nothing but a pervasive calm and an infinite certitude in the inherent goodness of the Universe. Stepping to the dais, I had known this would happen, and I felt that I was finally ready for it.

Like a snorkeler, I swam in a lazy circle through the air, noticing all the activity in church below. I floated outside the building to the front lawn. I saw my family coming up the walk in a messy procession, as if stumbling out of the car after a long and busy day at the beach. Peter and Carmen were there and Rafe chewed gum with his eight-year-old big-kid wonky teeth. There were others, less distinct—my father, George, my Auntie Susan, siblings, and cousins. I tried to notice details, something I could grasp and remember to corroborate that this had been real when I went back into my body.

At the same time, I acknowledged to myself that I didn't need proof. The experience was enough. And in that moment, I had to acknowledge that I might never go back to my body. That idea arrived with no panic, sadness, or regret.

There was no light, no voice. There wasn't joy so much as inordinate calm. All sound had been turned off. I could see everyone, but not hear what they were saying, and I just watched everything with a gaze of permeating love.

I felt, I suppose, a little detached. But more like my brain was infinite: tapped into every other consciousness, ego-boundaries collapsed like flimsy walls, at One with all living things.

And then I noticed a bit of will, a little quite-specific-Mollyness, snagging on my spirit. That little bit of Molly gripped onto the inchoate material of my spirit like a rough pinky fingernail catching cloth.

I could choose to go On, or go Back. I knew if I went Back it meant continued suffering, and sickness, and fear, and uncertainty about dying and leaving my loves if I took the longer road of an earthly life.

I went Back.

The next thing I knew, I woke up inside my body, still within the dream. Peter had come inside the church by then and he hovered over me and searched my face, as if he knew what had happened. He didn't press or pry, but let it be.

I noticed Vanessa, one of the teenagers from the orphanage, at my side. In real, waking life, Vanessa had a few years earlier suffered been through a psychotic break so severe they thought she had schizophrenia. But with careful tending and good trauma-informed care, she was restored to herself. Though even after her break, she remained dreamy and distant, a person who seemed like she was living between worlds.

In the dream, Vanessa sat next to me and held my hand with motherly care. I tenderly put my hand up to her face and patted it, and we just knew, together, what I had been through. That's when I became aware of the most divine joy flooding every ounce of my body.

The joy was so strong, it woke me up.

I lay there in bed in the dark, next to Peter. The soles of my feet and my palms were tingling—no, *pouring out*—what felt like molecules of airborne gold. My belly was both light and heavy, spilling over waterfalls of joy. I didn't want to move. I felt like Something was working on me, and in me, and moving through me, searching and clearing me, and I didn't want to disturb its work.

I wondered if I was being miraculously healed of my back pain.

After about, I don't know, five minutes or three years, I decided to move a little bit. There was some of the old twinging in my back. I figured, well, no, I wasn't miraculously healed. But somehow, it didn't matter. I'd been changed. I'd been given a gift that no one and nothing could take away.

Later that day, I reported for duty at the hospital. They handed me a Bingo sheet of medical chores and asked me to work my way down it: blood pressure check, heart monitor, blood draw. And at the end, a chest X-ray. Each time the nurses and phlebotomists and X-ray techs looked at the sheet, they expressed surprise the doctor had ordered an X-ray. "But you're so young!" the refrain went, adding, "That's for older folks, to make sure they don't have pneumonia before going under anesthesia."

"It's what the doctor ordered," I repeated, shrugging.

Later that afternoon, as I was wrestling a hundred pieces of Holy Week liturgy into place on my Mac, my phone rang. It was not the hospital. It was the beloved and feared Dr. Emsbo, my six-foot-tall, thin, cool, and Nordically beautiful primary care doctor.

Beloved, because she was super smart, and for years, had been extremely patient with me as we discussed my self-diagnosed wrist cancer and other intermittent symptoms of mortality.

Feared, because every time I saw her, she would inevitably and unsmilingly remind me that I needed to lose five to ten pounds to be maximally healthy.

Today, on the phone, she was the one who was afraid. I could hear it in her voice, her Nordic cool shaken, peppering me with questions. "The chest X-ray turned up a mass. It's pretty big. Have you had a bad cold this winter? Have you ever had pneumonia? I can't remember how much you smoked in your twenties. And you were raised with smokers, right?"

Ever the pastor, when she sounded so alarmed, I wanted to calm *her* down. I felt that nothing could possibly be wrong with my lungs. I had just started swimming, and I was in the best shape of my life. I had no cough at all. "Are you sure it wasn't mayo from someone's sandwich smearing the film?" I joked.

"Molly," she cut me off. "I've ordered a CT scan for tomorrow at the hospital. After the radiologist reads it, you'll meet with a pulmonologist."

"Does it have to be tomorrow?" I asked. "It's Holy Week. Maybe it can wait till after Easter?"

"No. This has to happen now."

The bald fact that I might have cancer was suddenly overshadowed by a more alarming thought. "Does this mean I have to postpone my back surgery?"

"Yes," she said simply, no softening of the blow.

"Fuck." I'd started the day filled with a mysterious golden light. How could things be going so badly wrong? I wanted to weep. Too stunned to be scared yet about the mass, I was wrecked at the thought of having to endure more physical pain right when healing was almost within my grasp.

Then and now, a big part of my life's spiritual work has been getting okay with being inside my current earthly vehicle, with all its quirks and frailties and limitations and particularities. That work became harder when my vehicle broke down by the side of the road, steaming like a cartoon jalopy. As I've done when my actual car breaks down, I just wanted to sit on the curb and cry. I didn't yet realize that the six months of unremitting back pain had been an emergency flare that would save my life.

I'm not much of a student of Christian history, but my friend Mary Luti has taught me a lot about the saints and mystics over the years. She reminded me recently that their lives were as marked by suffering and even physical pain as by divine illumination. She offered me this litany of woe about some of the best-known saints, with typical Mary Luti sparkle and snark:

> *Thomas Aquinas, the prolific author and founding father of Catholic theology, had a blazing mystical encounter with God, after which he stopped writing. He said of his work, 'it's all straw.' Three months later, he died.*
>
> *St. Francis's friends grew tired of his quirks and his radicalism and, toward the end of his life, began to reject him. His health failed. One fiery night in prayer on a mountain, seraphim lasered Jesus's own wounds onto his frail body.*
>
> *The Little Flower, St. Thérèse of Lisieux, whose simple, practical spiritual path has become known as "The Little Way," often referred to herself as a grain of sand, "always littler, lighter, in order to be lifted more easily by the breeze of love." She died at twenty-four of tuberculosis, which had a companion element of spiritual torment while she felt the absence of God. Nonetheless, during her final agony, she kept repeating phrases like, 'I love you, God,' and 'I do not regret having surrendered myself to Love,' until she could no longer manage a breath.*

As I kept reading, I was reminded of my parishioner Liz, struggling mightily to feel the presence of God as Mary ended:

Before St. Theresa of Ávila had her spiritual flowering, she spent thirty years—thirty!—watching the clock while praying and feeling nothing. That she kept showing up anyway is remarkable, and it tells us some important things about the interior life—it's not all sweetness and light, love is often more a matter of the will than a feeling, the divine absence can be terribly painful, and prayer is nine-tenths perseverance.

If the saints, mystics, and martyrs suffered so brutally amid their encounters with God, did I really think non-saintly, quite ordinary Molly would get to start the day enrobed in gold and carry on without any further divine meddling before making supper that night? Why would God only show up as a divine Percocet, making life ever better and easier, or at least pain-free?

The ferocious modern mystic Annie Dillard reminds us that God's first knock at the door is sometimes pain and danger. She wrote in *Teaching a Stone to Talk*, "The churches are children playing on the floor with their chemistry sets, mixing up a batch of TNT to kill a Sunday morning. It is madness to wear ladies' straw hats and velvet hats to church; we should all be wearing crash helmets. Ushers should issue life preservers and signal flares; they should lash us to our pews."

The lot of us spend a good portion of our lives *trying*. Trying to stuff or starve, pamper or power-lift our bodies into a more acceptable form, or numb them into feeling less. Some of us try to please God or please stand-ins for God: dead parents, difficult partners, society at-large. We think we can work or will ourselves with what Anne Lamott calls our "tiny little control issues" into a superior spiritual state.

It turns out the mystical life is less about control than surrender, less about lying on our little beds trying to send our spirits out of our bodies, and more about learning how to be fully in our bodies. Less about trying to summon God than about leaving ourselves open to God's arrival, however painful or frightening.

To misquote Einstein, we have a choice: to live as if everything were a message from God, or nothing is. Extraordinary messages from God crash into our lives, both disorienting and radically reorienting us in ways that make for the juiciest living.

When I hung up the phone after talking with Dr. Emsbo, I could feel every cell in my body, wildly alive and singing. I wasn't yet sure what genre the song was: death metal or praise music, but I knew both would be necessary for wholehearted spiritual living.

The next morning, my cancer journey took off at warp speed.

And two weeks later, my back pain was entirely gone.

Chapter 3

THE SUPERPOWER
OF VULNERABILITY

From about kindergarten until I reached age twenty-five—what I then believed was early spinsterhood—I was a hopeless romantic. I was forever in the throes of an unrequited crush, either pining away for someone who didn't know I existed or falling in love with someone who was marginally interested, but emotionally unavailable. At some point, probably in mid-seminary when my prefrontal cortex finally snapped into place, I saw the pattern: as long as I loved someone impossible, I wouldn't have to be truly vulnerable.

This might have had something to do with my early life. I was one of six kids in a big, chaotic, blended family—the one who tried to worry our collective parents the least. The A-student, the nerd, the good doobie, the one allergic to lying and shoplifting, the one who didn't drink or smoke until college. When I did take a ditch day in high school, it was to go to the Museum of Fine Arts and soak up beauty or walk the Freedom Trail in Boston. I often felt like both my parents thought I really lived with the other one, and when I was in their home, I was a polite and generally helpful houseguest, one they could more or less forget about because she knew how to take care of herself.

Strong and sensible, I still saw myself as inherently vulnerable, in part because I was so wholeheartedly emotional, always in the grip of enormous feelings that threatened to undo me. I could do deep relationships, though. When it came to best friends, I was a serial monogamist. Into each chapter of my life, God sent phenomenal friends who first made me feel safe, and then made me feel brave. As we've grown up, they have taken a forever place in the pantheon of my heart: from Leslie, who bought shy, nerdy me a Snickers bar at church camp on my twelfth birthday; to fierce and fabulous Aisha in college, whose soft underbelly only I got to see; to Supercatholicfragilistic Sarah in divinity school, who both loved astrology and gave side-eye to the Pope; and finally, Sue, who I met when I arrived at First Church Somerville. She became my work wife and is straight-up the best human I know. My besties are gorgeous. They are brilliant. They are kind. And they are taken.

But in romantic love, it turns out I wanted to protect my heart and not deal with the inconvenience of having to check in on another person's preferences or needs. Which meant I could be quite lonely, especially when my current local best friend was inconveniently unavailable because she was grounded, or studying abroad in Kenya, or had been brainwashed by a Christian cult (yes, that happened).

Maybe having best friends would be enough in life, I decided, especially when a particularly rollicking Old Testament study group at Yale Divinity School churned the seven of us into a salty, smart gang that included my bestie Sarah; her boyfriend Nathan; Bob and Nance, whose angel-faced Midwestern niceness belied a wickedly sacrilegious sense of humor; Sherry of the long wild tresses; and her roomie Peter.

Peter Baskette was cute and nice. Too nice to be boyfriend material. He had a longtime college sweetheart, which you'd think would make him catnip for me—but God must have put scales over my eyes. It's all in the timing.

After two years of friend-zoning, one steamy June when class was out, Peter and I took a road trip to Boston and found ourselves, weirdly, hot for each other. What started as a wildly romantic summer hookup quickly became more when I confessed my love for him in a thunderstorm of biblical proportions as we got soaked in the garlic patch of a Rhode Island farm.

Now that I was past the initial terror of having my feelings actually requited, I still had to spend a long season of negotiating how to be my strong self *and also* be in a deeply mutual intimate relationship. It was dreadfully vulnerable work. Through it, Peter, with a few exceptions as he dealt with demons of his own, was steady and patient through my tears and wrecking-ball behavior. When my adult-child-of-alcoholics divaness drove me into stormy seas, he helped me navigate back into safe harbor.

Marriage didn't complete us, but it was part of helping us heal from our past as we renegotiated patterns and deepened our friendship.

Four or five years in, as we found ourselves in calmer waters, I increasingly took on the role of chief optimist and rudder of the family domain while he worked more and more intensely outside of the home in provider mode. His work claimed the lion's share of his energy and it had become my habit to protect him as much as possible from the vicissitudes of our family emotional system. It seemed only fair, after how I felt he rescued me from the stormy waters of emotional highs and lows, that I rescue him right back.

Every marriage—like every family, workplace, and other ecosystem of relationships—has roles we fall into. They can help stabilize the naturally chaotic vagaries of life. Unless our roles become rigid. When we can't take turns doing the hard thing, when one of us doesn't have the luxury of falling apart or have access to a whole range of feelings, that's when roles effectively disable everyone in the system.

To always be the "strong" one stops your partner from discovering their own strength. To do the emotional heavy lifting in the relationship, you might forget how to experience and metabolize your own feelings in real time. In healthy relationships, people take turns and try on different roles as life introduces new dynamics (note: this theory also applies to laundry, dishes, and yardwork, ye heteros).

On that fateful Thursday before Palm Sunday when I hung up the phone with Dr. Emsbo, I immediately called Peter at work. How do you break it to your spouse that the long, luscious life you had planned together might be going sideways, fast?

As casually as I could, I said, "Um. They gave me an X-ray today, to prep for the back surgery. Only they found, totally unrelated, a mass in my lung."

Less casually, he responded, "Fuck. FUCK. FUCKFUCKFUCKFUCK-FUCK." Act 5, scene 372 of the drama of marriage had begun.

Since Peter was freaking out, I had to remain calm. It was my job. But I was instantly resentful of my instinct to calm him down. Was I not even going to allow myself to fall apart about the thing that might be silently killing me?

For both of our survival, I stepped into another role, asking him for what *I* needed. And the drama changed. "Can I be the one to freak out about this thing happening in my own body? And can you come home right now?" I asked.

"Yes," he said. "And yes."

I hung up, and in a haze of lizard-brain urgency, my body led me straight outside in front of the church. It was the Thursday before Palm Sunday, that time in New England when the sun is trying to shine bravely in an intuition of spring, but winter is still cracking the whip.

Three of my church members, Jen, Cindy, and Liz, were handing out treat-stuffed Easter eggs to commuters, inviting them to Holy Week worship. It was our long-standing hospitality practice as a city church, equal parts terrifying and hospitable to antisocial Bostonians. Four-year-old Carmen, our church's secret weapon for evangelism, was hanging out with them. She never missed a chance to melt strangers into friends: people dropped like flies before her tiny, gentle imperiousness. Plus, she got to stuff Easter eggs in her pocket when nobody was looking.

My body moving of its own accord, I walked right up to them. They were probably expecting the Pastor Molly they'd known for years by then: cheerful, confident, in-charge Molly. Instead, I squeaked out of a dry mouth, "Can you stop a moment? Can you come to the church steps? I have something to tell you."

We pulled back from the curb, our neighbors probably sighing with relief to have dodged those sweet but insistent progressive Christians for once.

"I just talked to my doctor. They found a mass in my lung. Will you pray for me?"

In high-anxiety and high-emotion moments, pastors need to follow two rules. Number one: breathe. Number two: don't let other people's freaking out freak you out. For years, I had been modeling the non-anxious presence for my congregation. And now, Jen and Cindy and Liz returned the favor.

They took my hands and they prayed for me. Carmen, oblivious to what we were saying but drawn to the spiritual energy, did slow, lazy circles around us, holding fistfuls of eggs.

For nearly forty years, self-sufficiency, optimism, and the power of the hustle moved me through an elite public high school and two Ivy League schools and well into a career. My brand was strength and success (Why yes, I *am* an Enneagram 3. Thanks for asking).

But it turned out that what I needed to survive the next chapter was not strength. Or rather, I now needed a kind of upside-down strength: learning how to be vulnerable and trust that the net of community that God and I had woven together over many decades would hold. Hustle was only going to get me so far.

Things moved fast after I saw the pulmonologist five days before Easter. The trinity of women who prayed for me that first evening kept my news confidential, so the church as a whole wouldn't be robbed of Easter's joy in their worry for me. But soon after Holy Week, I told my people and then went into Brigham and Women's hospital for a lobectomy, where they cut away half my lung.

It took them weeks to figure out just what the blue, perfectly round lump was. The news finally came back that it was Ewing's sarcoma, an aggressive cancer that usually strikes teenage boys in their long bones and requires a long protocol of chemo. I was one of only twelve people in the world who had ever had Ewing's first appear in their lung. My dad joked at the time that I was breaking news in the elevators at Dana Farber Cancer Institute. "We have an actual primary lung Ewing's sarcoma! I was behind her in the cafeteria today. She got the tater tots!"

Two weeks after the news, Peter and I were on our way to Playa del Carmen in Mexico. His sister, also named Carmen, had booked us into an all-inclusive resort; my brother Jesse bought our plane tickets. All we had to do was pack bathing suits and go. We spent long hours snorkeling and snarfing beautiful fruit plates and making love, thinking only about what to eat next or what midnight creature was scampering across the roof of our palapa hut. Then just as suddenly, we'd be walking down the pedestrian mall toward dinner when I would stop and finger the scarves for sale, wondering if I should buy one for impending baldness. I realized my whole life was about to change in a way I couldn't yet imagine.

Two weeks later chemo began. And two weeks after that, with Swiss precision, I began to lose my hair. One day, it was just a few strands. The next, I was a dandelion gone to seed in a strong breeze.

I decided to jump in rather than get pushed off the diving board. We called my friend Jason, bestie Sue's husband, a minister, and likewise a person who knows how to save the day with sarcasm. He came with beer and hair clippers. Together, he and eight-year-old Rafe shaved me bald. It was very empowering for Rafe to take from me all at once what chemo was taking in painful spurts. Then Jason turned the clippers on Rafe, for a mohawk, and then on himself. He spent the next nine months in the solidarity of baldness.

I loved my new look. I had a GI Jane toughness. With the pounds I had lost since surgery and hollowed-out cheeks I'd never had, I felt like Linda Hamilton in *Terminator 2*. But in the days to come, my stubble started growing in patchily, and I looked more like someone who'd been living in a bunker for decades.

Losing my hair was one of the hardest parts of chemo. A Leo, my hair was always my glory, my armor. Becoming bald was a deep spiritual lesson in shedding my own Samson-like strength. It was an opportunity to stop hiding, to be seen with all my flaws and frailty. Until then, I'd been able to calculate the degree to which I would disclose my illness. But this was a whole new level of being-human-while-pastoring.

And then there was the practical question of learning how to be bald: What to wear up there? How could I learn to tie that scarf I bought in Playa del Carmen so I would look more like Frida Kahlo and less like Yul

Brynner doing drag badly? I fussed with wigs (itchy and annoying), then decided on a vintage Sophia Loren look, all big sunglasses and silk scarves. Until one day at the playground, a stiff breeze flung the scarf off my head and revealed my naked dome. As I ran after it, everyone politely pretended not to watch.

After that, I started going bald around my urban village on purpose. I took to watching people's faces. Did they flinch when they looked at me? Would their faces sink into pity, or fear? I felt like a mirror for them, or a cautionary tale: one minute, a healthy, vigorous thirty-nine-year-old; the next, someone staring into the abyss.

Many kind adults assured me that I looked radiant, like a Buddhist nun, that my head was beautifully shaped and my eyes "popped." I didn't need them to damn me with strange praise. I just wanted them to be able to match the solemnity of what was happening without trying to bright-side it. That was Carmen's role, who daily would say to me, while rubbing my head, "You are the most *beautiful* bald momma."

In fact, I far preferred the reaction of children to my baldness. Children can't do anything other than tell the truth, or, more likely, show the truth on their faces.

The kids in my life would first be surprised, but after an invitation almost always wanted to touch my head. They'd approach it as if it were a wild animal, which maybe it was, in a way. They touched first gently and then with more confidence.

And then it was done. They'd accepted the new reality and become like my own children, incorporating my baldness into our everyday life, Rafe telling loud bald jokes and elbowing me in the side, or Carmen singing songs with a shaky vibrato. "Does she look in the mirror and wonder, 'Who is that woman?'" she trilled.

One thing I definitely didn't realize was just how much more bald it was possible to get. My Phinney eyebrows, wee to begin with, fled the scene. I looked like a sinuous genderfluid alien until the ladies at Sephora took pity on me and showed me how to paint them back on.

Seven weeks in, I still had a few eyelashes to bat, but soon even those were gone.

By late July, a dangerously low white blood cell count put me in the hospital for a week with very little to do but stare at myself in the mirror opposite the hospital bed. The dissonance between the Molly-Strong that had carried me so far in life and the Molly-Bald that I had become was starting to resolve. *I am a cancer patient*, I realized. I acted like one. I felt like one. And now I looked like one.

This was an important spiritual step for me. This reality had to lock in at the most highly authorized levels of my being. Sometimes denial is necessary, even lifesaving. But too much, for too long, keeps us from really getting to the nourishing marrow of what our lives can teach us, how the unwanted can transform us.

Last of all, I lost the hair down there. I was in permanent, chemo-induced menopause. I'd come to terms with looking a lot older, very fast. But suddenly, there was a part of me that looked, *ahem*, alarmingly young. In the course of a month, I had gone from Mother to confusingly *both* Maiden and Crone.

I worried about what that would mean for Peter's and my sex life. Was he ready for an encounter that might conjure images of internet porn search terms like "BARELY LEGAL is she REALLY 18???"

To my husband's credit, when he saw me naked, he didn't bat a single eyelash (how I begrudged him those eyelashes). He didn't make jokes, betraying his own discomfort. He told me that I was as sexy and beautiful to him as ever, and set out to prove it, giving me back the dignity that had been robbed from me during the many medical procedures and side effects that are the collateral damage of chronic illness.

While every cancer patient's libido and sex life are different, we had nary a hiccup in our marital bed, the benefit of years of practice with each other. Even with these changes, we had an unerring sense of each other. For this intimacy, I was then, and remain, deeply grateful. Cancer, and marriage, is hard enough without giving up orgasms.

I recovered and went home from the hospital just in time to go to church camp—my happiest place in the world—for the week. The place I had grown into so much of myself. No starring roles this time. I was just another conferee at Family Camp, where I spent most of the time taking naps and shivering off random fevers while kind people took my kids swimming or to arts and crafts. At worship, on the last night of camp, I gave this halting little sermon to our crew:

> *One thing I've learned over the years is that at Silver Lake, God can give you a clear idea of yourself. Usually, the clear idea that God gives you is that you are beautiful and strong. But sometimes the idea that God gives you is that you are beautiful and weak. Sometimes God takes away our abilities so that we can give other people an opportunity to serve us. That's what happened to me this week. I was not able to be strong in the ways I usually count on being, at Silver Lake or anywhere, and you noticed, and you quietly stepped in, and were servants of Jesus, for me and for my children. I want to thank you for that.*

A few weeks after coming home from camp, I stepped out of medical leave for a moment to be in the worship service at my church. I wanted to lay a special blessing on my friend Lupita, visiting from Mexico, the director of the orphanage there that had made us friends. It had only been three months since I stopped officially working and I was amazed at how little I already felt like a minister. Instead, I felt like a frail, teary, distracted human. I heard God saying, "That's more like it."

I worried that my people, my cherished, beautiful people who (I hoped) still had a few illusions about me, couldn't handle seeing their faith leader skinny and sick and not lose heart. I had forgotten how many of them had stared into their own abysses. They didn't need me to be *anything*.

After church that day, I wrote in my journal, "Right now it's not the fear of treatment that is getting to me. It's—finally—the fear of dying. I always say that one of my two jobs as a pastor is to prepare people to die, myself included. And my other job is to prepare people to live. There are so many things that we just don't understand, rich things about the world, until we're initiated into the sorrow of them. I'm so glad many other people have gotten there first, my guides. 'As much as sorrow has carved out your being,' wrote Kahlil Gibran, 'that's how much joy you can contain.'"

The consequence of not being able to show all of your parts to at least one other human—your abject fears, your addictions, your disordered desires, your compulsive thoughts, your legitimate emotional or physical or sexual needs, and more—is a bifurcation of the soul. Cancer came just in time for me to call a halt to the building out of a massive ego infrastructure. Our church was growing into a wild, creative, and vibrant community and getting a name for itself: the cool, young church with the Drag Gospel Festival. I was also getting a bit of a name for myself and starting to believe my own press.

Then, all of a sudden, I had to contend with not just my church but the whole world seeing another me: that lonely little girl terrified of being weak and depending on others who might just disappoint her if she had the courage to need them.

Luckily, my church had a lot of practice in loving people not just when but *because* they showed up whole, integrated, messy, with all of their pieces and parts on display.

A while ago, I wrote about First Church Somerville's long-standing practice of putting a different layperson on the mic each week to confess their sins in worship (*Standing Naked Before God*). This is not as scandalous as it sounds—mostly, what people confess to is garden-variety selfishness, myopia, jealousy, or cowardice.

But importantly, it's an exercise in vulnerability: in showing each other our wounds and our weakness, so we can be whole and wholehearted, together.

When I was their pastor, I noticed that at this urban church rife with people struggling with substance abuse, mental health crises, debt, and poverty, people were more "well" than the fine-looking folks I had known in suburban churches I'd served. I believe it had everything to do with our culture of offering confession and then receiving grace from the embodied Christ manifest in the people in the pews, their peers. We preached that grace, and we practiced it. We were a living reminder that the "fully human/fully God" rabbi we followed was vulnerable every step of the way. He was born into poverty and barely escaped infanticide. He died young by state violence. And even when he was resurrected, he rose *with* his wounds.

We hate being vulnerable because we don't entirely know who we can trust not to deliver a killing blow. We develop strategies and habits that we keep employing long after we've reached adulthood, found friendships or relationships that are safe and nurturing, or created a family life that treasures real intimacy and mutual aid—but still, old instincts persist.

Every one of us will be wounded by life. None of the armor we have devised—not wealth, not professional expertise, not emotional shutdown—not backup plans for our backup plans—can protect us.

To be entirely seen, to be naked before one another and before God, is what I most need, and what I am entirely afraid of. We fear being judged and shunned for our badness because to be shunned, separated from the protective herd, is death.

In the white, upper-middle-class, suburban church where I served before First Church Somerville, in a bedroom community north of Boston with Puritan roots, there was a strong taboo against "airing your dirty laundry" at church. If people divorced, they disappeared. If their difficult children grew into wayward teens, they likewise faded away rather than go to their spiritual community for support.

When people from my congregation found themselves going off the rails in one way or another, they were sometimes shunned and only spoken about in whispers. Since it's easier for me to love an underdog, I was naturally drawn to them.

Mike was one of them. He also happened to be my favorite person in the church. He was hilarious, smart, and self-deprecating, without a trace of the low-key chauvinism I was always bumping into as female clergy. He was an adoring father and a tender husband. He was in a leadership position at the church when he came to me and told me the truth: the Feds had found child pornography on his computer at work.

He was charged with a felony, but since he didn't have a prior record and, with the privilege that comes with being an upper-middle-class white man, he was released on bail while awaiting trial. His wife, understandably, kicked him out, and he got fired. He moved into a motel as his life caved in around him. We went for a walk around a nearby farm, and as we moved past a riot of spring flowers, my newborn baby boy, Rafe, in my arms, Spirit led me to ask a question I wasn't sure I wanted an answer to.

"Mike? Were there any active victims?" He knew what I meant. Was there anyone he had perpetrated abuse against in embodied life, rather than by passively consuming child porn? He said, unequivocally, no.

But a week later, he asked me to go for another walk. And this time, he told me the truth. There was a victim: his child's best friend, whose parents were their close friends. Eager to practice this thing called "restorative justice" that I was learning about, I thought it could be helpful for Mike to confess directly to his friends before going to the police—spiritually helpful for Mike, and his friends, to connect directly rather than through lawyers or courts, a beginning at making amends. We met in a therapist friend's office as a safe, neutral place for the conversation.

The *idea* of restorative justice, and true restorative justice, are not the same. It turned out to be an ignorant and clumsy move. I had no childcare, and baby Rafe was a distraction. I was not a skilled enough guide in the conversation, which was abrupt and devastating, as Mike told his friends how he had used their trust to his advantage, to hurt and manipulate their child in the most devastating way a parent can imagine. Nineteen years later, the look on their faces is branded on my brain.

Still, it took an enormous amount of courage for him to face his victims before any pressure from the court made him do so. He wept, and they wept. Their friendship was shattered. But in the days and weeks and years to come, I hoped that Mike's willingness to face them directly, offering them the dignity of honesty and accountability, showing up in his wholeness, would somehow allow them to be more whole after this shattering, refusing to damn themselves for what they had missed, and offering themselves grace as they learned how to parent their child into who they would become. Mike was more than the worst thing he had ever done, and maybe, in the mystery, that would help everyone involved be fully themselves in all their complexity.

In the years that followed, including a five-year stint in prison, Mike's initial willingness to face his victims made him better able to face the full reality of, and consequences for, what he had done without blaming or denying. This punishment, this pain, was an essential part of the cure. He was transferred to the facility with the most aggressive treatment for pedophilia, which involved, among other things, cultivating empathy for his victims, both the active and the passive. In the process, he humanized them—and himself.

He did the deep psychological work to understand his own motivations and compulsions so he could best them. For years, I went to visit him, even after I moved. We continued writing letters because he had no other pastor. When he was released, he moved to a town known for both its high concentration of sex offenders and a church that had turned its childlessness into a blessing for those offenders: a community where they would not be shunned or shamed but could help each other live more intentionally without doing further harm.

We lost touch a few years after his release. Then one day, I spotted him at IKEA, but he didn't see me. I was not ready for an encounter that day—and maybe he wasn't either. I hid behind a display of baskets. He was with a new partner. He looked happy and relaxed. They were shopping for lamps. There is more than one way to move into the light.

Having found such spiritual sustenance from visiting Mike in prison, I felt drawn to prison ministry as a piece of my parish ministry work. A local nonprofit paired me with Gloria, a longtime inmate at the women's correctional facility near my new home. When I first went to visit her, she was so starved for company that she poured out her whole story to me. Her early adult life had been predicated on being a mother, and a good one. She didn't feel safe in her marriage and, despite being very involved in her church, she didn't feel like she could talk to anyone about what was going on. Nor did her mental health providers correctly diagnose her escalating bipolar disorder. Unable to imagine any other kind of escape, she experienced a psychotic break in which she planned to kill both of her children with her husband's shotgun, and then take her own life. In heaven, she thought, they would be together, and out of danger.

One night, she did it. She shot and killed her older child before turning to the younger, who in the dark confusion of emerging from sleep instinctively pushed the barrel of the gun aside. When Gloria then turned it on herself, it misfired.

The jury rejected the insanity defense and the judge sentenced her to life in prison. She had served nine years by the time I met her, a small, trim woman who talked somewhat slowly but whose eyes and manner barely contained the nervous energy that bubbled out of her.

Gloria knew what she had done, and faced it fully. She said to me over the overpriced M&Ms and pretzels I got from the canteen, "My crime *is* my punishment. I've lost both of my children: one by my own hand and one because of what I did to the other."

In the aftermath of such loss and trauma, she had become a mother figure to many of the women in prison, finding purpose in loving and nurturing them in the absence of the children God had originally sent. The DA called this impulse pathological and, over the years of her parole hearings, cited it as a reason to keep her incarcerated.

With Gloria's permission, I reached out to her surviving daughter. Like visiting Mike and Gloria, spending time with Faith was among the most poignant ministry I have ever done. Faith's grief was complicated. She had maintained through the trial that Gloria was an excellent mother and understood that her mother was a victim as well in all that had unfolded. But she didn't know if she could forgive her. She made a third way for herself, finding a wary détente, visiting her mother in prison occasionally and even bringing her own child, who I had the blessing of baptizing in a private ceremony, since her own church had shed her along with her mother.

I went to two parole hearings for Gloria, and at the second one, I was allowed to speak.

> I have become convinced over the course of our many conversations about her crime and its aftermath, that Gloria was doing all the necessary inner work to understand what she had done and take full responsibility for it. She is truly repentant and her commitment to God and to her faith is genuine and full. She has worked hard while serving her time to prepare herself for a new kind of life when she is released, gaining knowledge and confidence by attaining her undergraduate degree and practical skills by pursuing a cosmetology degree. She has worked hard to become and remain emotionally and spiritually healthy through therapy and deep spiritual practices of personal prayer, spiritual direction, and attendance at Mass. These are tools that will help her to re-orient and become a well-adjusted, responsible, mature, and contributing member of society when she is finally released.

Gloria was granted parole after nineteen years in prison. We talk often on the phone. She really wanted to come to my church after her release, and did make it once, but her life grew small in prison and it is hard to start over again in the big, unpredictable outer world. I suspected she would need a stronger and more anonymous container than our intimate, messy, raucous UCC; she has found it in a kind Catholic community and deep friendship with a nun there.

I think often about Mike and Gloria. Their humility, their gratitude, their willingness to talk about what really matters. They are so clear on what their spiritual work is, and that the worst thing they had ever done has nonetheless brought them into deep communion with God and other vulnerable souls for mutual healing.

Here's what I keep thinking: What if church was a safe enough place for Mike to tell someone about his urges before he ever acted on them? What if there had been less of a taboo in faith communities on getting mental health support or talking about partner violence before it came to a crisis for Gloria?

My current church in Berkeley is a mix of my suburban church (no dirty laundry!) and Somerville (no closets here!). I still find full-sun Californians can have a hard time opening up. When people are asked to give testimonies in my church, they often say they don't have "just the right story," by which I suspect they mean a story that makes them out to be a deep and humble hero, which entirely defeats the purpose. Even our everyday lives can be the stuff of spiritual transformation; we teach each other as much by our frailty as our virtue.

But when people do speak up, watch out. As they give oxygen to their stories about psychiatric hospitalizations, early abuse, or relationship turmoil, they give us access to our own tenderest places. Amid this unspooling of messy interior lives, a retired public health nurse started a mental health ministry that has grown to include almost half of our congregation. At least 150 people have trained to be mental health companions, shared leadership in the mental health spiritual support group, or otherwise leveled up in mental health support. There are no leaders and no "clients" in this ministry; mental health is something we all have and all need support for. The more we can make church a place to demystify and destigmatize mental illness as well as disordered desires, the more we can help each other heal and do less harm.

Soon after I moved to Berkeley, a small, older-membership church invited me to come talk to them about church renewal where the practice of testimony was central. Because good church is not a spectator sport, I put the folks in my workshop to work. I said "Let's go around the room. Name one thing that is making you feel vulnerable right now in your life." The first person to my left was a man. He said, "I'm not feeling vulnerable!" with false heartiness. I didn't press him. I moved on to the second man, "What's making you feel vulnerable this week?" He answered, "Vulnerability" and got an empathetic chuckle around the room.

On the second pass, I pushed them deeper: tell about something bad you did when you were fifteen. One person told us about stealing gum. Someone else told us about stealing a boyfriend. Now we were getting somewhere!

Then my host, the woman who had originally invited me to teach, spoke up. She had worked at the church years earlier and had long-standing relationships with the people there, but they had never heard this story. With her voice shaking, she told us about the violence with which her first marriage had ended. She found new love in the kind music director—but she confessed that she found herself immediately telling little lies to him, to please him, to make herself into more of who she thought he wanted. After years of lying to her ex-husband, she found it hard to break the habit. She was ashamed of herself for lying to him and for betraying herself again. And then she described how God gave her the courage to confess her lies to him. He forgave her. They married. And twenty years later, here he was in my workshop, sitting by her side as she told this story, both of them weeping Holy Spirit tears, as much in love as ever.

When she was done, silence reigned. Not a stunned silence, or an embarrassed one. A holy one.

Now I invited the people in the room to go around again. This time, I said, "Tell about a person you have hurt." And they opened up like flowers before one another, these people who had known each other for years, without knowing each other at all. One woman spoke about making her fifteen-year-old feel like crap about himself for getting bad grades. Another spoke about what she did to her kids while she was still drinking. And when we got to the end of a circle, a man who had passed entirely on the first round could not speak, but indicated he had something to say. We waited patiently while he found his voice. He told us about his son's death by suicide thirty years earlier, about his sorrow and guilt that he hadn't tried harder to hear him and save him. He wept openly.

The people in the circle didn't cheapen his confession by brushing it aside or offering false comfort. They just held him tight, and let him cry, and no one looked away. And I knew in that moment, that even if that particular church closes, it will never, ever die.

Chapter 4

THE BODY AND THE BLOOD

In the middle of a heat wave during the second month of chemo, my family and I escaped to the home and flower farm of our dear friends Leslie and Sam in Western Massachusetts. I wanted to spend time with my kids and feel like a normal mom—worn to a thread by the day and the heat and the demands of childrearing—instead of feeling like a sick mom—worn to a thread by chemotherapy, only seeing my children for half an hour on my bed in the evening like some kind of invalid Victorian noble.

Les and Sam's farm was a refuge and respite. Les, my church camp bestie, had taken seriously Christianity's calls to Earth care and profligate generosity. She and her husband, Sam, bought a piece of land in a little valley in the crook of the South River and built a small, nearly self-sustaining house. They put in an orchard and a garden meant to feed their family and many friends all year. They regularly invited others to share the land for free: young adults trying out farming, local immigrant laborers, and even the Trump fans next door who needed extra space for their beloved llamas.

Whenever we arrived at the land, the littles would immediately jump on the trampoline, tiny Adams and Eves, naked and unashamed. They'd chase chickens, swim, cover themselves in river mud, fly high on the tree swing, and check on the apple trees we had planted together over their placentas when they were young (among phrases that have been uttered at the farm, "Carmen, my placenta is bigger than your placenta!").

When we visit, the Baskettes bring a little meat or fish and a bottle of wine. The garden supplies everything else: curried potato salad with fresh snap peas and parsley, cold borscht, and gigantic salads. The crickets put us to sleep and the birds wake us up. It is the embodiment of healing, which is why we went to visit after pretty much every consecutive chemo poisoning.

The problem was, my body refused to cooperate. Early July's chemo set off a fireworks display of terrible side effects. All the early-onset ones came back with a vengeance and brought some malicious new ones. Mouth sores galore! Thrush! And terrible, terrible reflux.

These things sound harmless enough when you assign *names* to them in sweet little twelve-point Garamond type, but I assure you: while no one symptom was life-threatening and I did not puke even once, the constellation of chemo side effects, overlaid at specific points in the cycle with a chemical depression, was spirit-deadening and deeply discouraging.

I was supposed to exercise every day for its anticancer properties, but was exhausted and anemic, my heart gonging my body threateningly when I asked it to make any extra effort, my stomach a big bag of acid shooting Roman candles into my esophagus. Standing up made me dizzy and want to vomit. But every movement I could make to keep to the ambitious chemo schedule counted. So, the first morning of our visit, before it got hot, Sam watched our kids while Peter and I went for a slow, country walk.

We went down the road, crossed the river, and up a short, steep dirt road, past foxglove and mallow and wild raspberry brambles to where the sun was just coming over the ridge. It was a clear day, and stunningly beautiful. It was the kind of image good for saving for guided meditations, when the voice on the recording says, "Go to the safest place you know."

But I couldn't go there, even though I *was* there. I was stuck in this increasingly compromised and kvetching body, and hot tears just started pouring out of it. "I thought cancer was supposed to make me more stripped down and spiritual, you know, burn away all the vices and the pettiness, and leave me this radiant creature who dispenses unassailable generous wisdom to everyone around me!

"Instead, all I can do is talk about my symptoms, obsess about medication, and ruminate on treatment cycles. All I can think about is how I'm going to get through the next fifteen minutes, whether it's time yet for Zantac or Neupogen or Miracle Mouthwash, L-Carnitine or Mesna or Tylenol. Whether I should try Ativan or Compazine or Marinol for the breakthrough nausea.

"And when I'm not thinking about *that*, I'm perseverating about chemo. In my mind's eye, I see the treatment center and my stomach fills with acid; I hear the voice of the *Chemo, My Friend CD* lady and want to throw up. And I'm only done with three of the fourteen treatments!"

Luckily, Peter, a very practical man who knows me very well, said, "Molly, this is what we're doing right now. It's not going to last forever. It is what it is, and you have to let go of any idea of producing anything out of this—wisdom, meaning. As for getting triggered, you just have to trick yourself. When you're not at the hospital, don't think about it. The night before, do what you need to do to get ready, and every alternate Tuesday, say 'Whoops! Oh, we're going to Dana Farber today!'" And as he steered me gently down the road, he kept making little jokes that he knew would make me laugh.

Christians are all about the body. Our theological word for it is *incarnation*, which sounds like "incantation," and probably not far off. What it literally, etymologically means, is that we are enfleshed, we are put into meat. *Somos carne!*

We say that if God took on a body in the form of Jesus, bodies must be inherently good, and we should celebrate the body: eating good food, making love, cuddling people or pets, swimming strong, or running fast.

The two primary Christian sacraments are about the body. Water pours over it in baptism and food goes into it in communion. We get the message. Spirit = good. Body = *also* good.

But when we're in pain, we naturally doubt this message. Chemo gave me a lot more compassion for old people, for people with chronic illnesses or chronic pain, for people who can't get out of the bed or the chair. For me, this was a temporary journey through disability, though I knew it would come back to collect me later in life. Helen, a disability rights activist in my church, says, "What's the difference between an abled person and a disabled person? Time."

The people who have already arrived into the difficulties of the body have to find a way to make peace with it for the long haul. Some of us can only do it in fifteen-minute increments before our next meltdown. Others let their compromised bodies become their spiritual teachers, taking lesson after lesson about resilience and gratitude. Still, others don't find peace in the pain, and this is no reflection on their character. It is just a hard fact of being human.

This year I buried my friend Jessie, who died of ALS a month shy of her fifty-first birthday. Since we were freshmen in college, Jessie had been a tiny five-foot fountain of joy and justice-doing. We were seniors at Dartmouth when we traveled to Daytona Beach for spring break to be on an MTV lip-synch game show. We lost, but she got the biggest audience applause line for turning out as a giant dancing condom to Salt-n-Pepa's "Let's Talk About Sex." She worked as a town manager and was a fearless advocate for the earth, for teachers, and for racial justice at every level of government.

Getting sick didn't change her; it just changed her delivery methods. Confined to a wheelchair, writing with her eyes through the magic of technology, she'd publish long, moving, often funny Facebook posts about everything from partisan politics to the flowers outside her window. Whenever I needed a smackdown for pettiness and irritation about my perfectly reasonable life, I'd steep myself in her words.

Jessie had ALS for nearly seven years before she decided her diminished body was just too tired to be alive anymore. It was time to stop nutrition and enter hospice. She texted me that she wanted to plan her memorial service. I asked her, among other things, "How did you have the courage to go on, after your diagnosis?"

She answered, "I've always been an active person who liked physical challenges. ALS was just a series of physical challenges. I took them one at a time, day by day. I almost enjoyed having to find solutions to unique problems. I had periods of depression, and medication helped. So did moving to be able to see friends. My friends made a huge difference in my life. They made sure that I continued to have fun and to laugh. Laughter made it tolerable. I never felt like I was alone."

In a poem she wrote called "The Floor Plan," she elegantly described the accommodations she had made for her disability with the last line that reads, "In the house of an ALS patient, the glass is half full, for otherwise it is too heavy to carry."

Spiritual people have for millennia incorporated bodily pain into their spiritual practices as a way of drawing close to the divine. Medieval monks were big on "mortification of the flesh." They knelt in prayer for hours on cold stone floors, wore hair shirts, and self-flagellated (maybe for the endorphin rush?).

On that golden walk with Peter in early summer, I felt as if my flesh had been mortified, but had not brought me any closer to God. I was experiencing a whole new level of obsession about my body that felt distinctly un-holy, all about me-me-me instead of all about God.

The morning and evening pill-taking, the afternoon shot self-injecting, the handwashing so my immunosuppressed self didn't pick up a bug that could escalate, fast. The amount of time I spent cleaning my teeth alone quintupled, easily, by edict of dentist and oncologist, because the mouth can welcome a whole-body infection in less time than it takes to say, "Circles small, gums and all."

There were moments when I felt like the Gnostics and the Platonists had it right: we are just inhabiting these meat suits for a while and someday will burst out of them, our purest spirit-bodies, to live with God forever. I didn't really *believe* that, but I sure did *feel* it.

And then, in a momentary escape from the present suffering, I would flash back to the previous summer, sitting on bestie Sarah's back deck in Napa, on sabbatical, eating local goat cheese and drinking wine that her friend made, wine with ten different flavors inside of it. That wine was intoxicating in more ways than one, and it was only possible *because* I was blessed with a body. They say the angels are jealous of us, because we have bodies. Remembering that wine, I know why.

In moments of pain and body-obsession, God whispered, "It will come back, Molly: your taste buds will come back, your esophagus will come back, peristalsis, and with it, so much of the joy whose lot is cast with them. All this raw body hurt will be like a bad dream." A number of the cancer survivors I talked to back then had a hard time recalling the details and the pain of treatment when it was over. They said it was like the pain of labor. The mind protects us by forgetting. God's gracious gift of amnesia.

Soon after that trip to the flower farm, our church's lovely support pastor who was filling in for me, Ian, preached about good bread. He is Irish, with a lilting brogue, and he took us into a story about his grandmother's scones. It was 85 degrees in the sanctuary, but all of a sudden, we all wanted hot, buttered scones. It's important that the bread in church be delicious, that we should want more and more. Why else would we be there?

Then together, Ian and I served good bread. It was a communion Sunday, and I was grateful to be helping because I wasn't allowed to hug people anymore, nor shake their hands, nor touch their upper arm in a gesture of affection, nor stand and talk to them for hours at coffee hour, the way I always had. My immunocompromised body wouldn't permit it.

But I could look them in the eye, and say their name, and hand out the good bread, the strong body of Jesus Christ. It was not a poor substitute. It *is* all that other embodied stuff, the affection, the touch, the deep and wordless communion of life to life. Baked into a morsel of bread, a part for the whole.

THE BODY AND THE BLOOD

After the fourth chemo cycle, my body broke even more.

The wooziness surged as I was getting my children's breakfast at a chemo-patient's pace, and I nearly fell, hitting my head on the counter. I knew it was time for my first blood transfusion.

This was not as simple an undertaking as you might think. Aside from worries about contamination, you can actually be allergic to blood that's not yours.

Then I remembered the final scene from the eighties movie, *Jesus of Montreal*. Spoiler alert: the main character, who plays Jesus in a community theater passion play, dies in a freak accident during a performance. He is brain dead, and they farm out his organs and his blood to dozens of people—his blood shed for the healing of all, his life force repurposed to save others.

Watching that scene taught me about the spiritual necessity, not of giving, but of receiving. No matter who the literal giver is, somehow the gift (incarnationally, incantationally) comes from the body of Christ.

Watching another human being's blood flow into your veins is trippy and beautiful. If it were a movie, it would be some kind of Euro art house flick, with a touching piano soundtrack. It's not much like a mother nursing her child—there is all the plastic, and the beeping, and the alcohol swabs—but it *is* like it: the raw power, of life joining to life, of strength to weakness. An impossibly red substance flows down through the cannula at an unhurried pace, a canal joining the wild river of a human vein, currents merging, communion. It's the opposite of chemo—the most natural thing in the world, someone's organically grown life force, shed for me.

I found myself wondering, *Who was this person who gave me their blood? What did they eat for breakfast the day they donated? What was their temperament—were they angry, happy, melancholy, gregarious, hungry? Male or female or a little bit of each or none of the above? Were they old or young, Black or brown or white? Did it even matter, since the bag told me everything I needed to know: that we all bleed red?* I lifted my hands up to the bag in blessing and gave thanks for this person who had given a little bit of their life for mine.

On the way home, I made Peter stop for pepperoni pizza, which I had a sudden craving for. I ate half of it, and some strawberry rhubarb crisp, and three chicken drumsticks. I hadn't eaten like that in months. I decided: whatever else my donor was, they were definitely hungry. And now their hunger was in me.

High on a hill in Somerville, less than a mile away from my old church, lives a sweet storefront church called Igreja Mr. Jesus. The tagline of the church is "There is Power in His Blood." Whenever I'd sit idling in traffic in front of that church, I used to pray for the people inside. What were their lives like? What kind of savior did they hope for, that their comfort lay in the assertion, "There is power in His blood"?

A couple of years after chemo, the church choir in Somerville learned that some of the songs they'd be singing for Good Friday were about the blood of Jesus. There was anxiety. There was grumbling. What is all the blood business anyhow? This is not our theology. We are not people of the blood. "We are people of the Word," they said. The nice, clean, tidy Word.

In church, we sometimes say, "In the beginning was the Word," referring to Jesus. We know that God called the worlds into being with words. It is *words* that have power, not blood.

All I know is, that day when I almost fainted and hit my head on the counter, I didn't need words. I needed blood.

Blood is transgressive and taboo. We need it desperately and yet we are afraid of it and disgusted by it. We don't have to remember far back to the misplaced panic over blood and other bodily fluids during the AIDS epidemic and for a long time afterward. It made lepers and untouchables of a whole generation of gay men and others.

Yet, blood is the great unifier. Women who live together bleed in sync. People who survive the same bloody trauma are bonded forever. Blood brothers are those who willingly unite their blood. Blood bonds and blood saves.

Jesus became a blood donor. The scripture says he "gave up" his spirit. He made a choice. He had one last drink, he said, "It is finished," he bowed his head and died. And when they pierced his side a moment later, blood and water poured out for the many, that they might live.

Jesus was an innocent, unarmed, brown man who allowed himself to be scapegoated and slaughtered by the state, for one reason and one reason only: to be the last scapegoat. He bled out so that the bloodletting might stop; so that not one more innocent might have to open a vein to feed the violence economy.

Look at your wrist, the place where the blood pulses near the skin. Think what a miracle you are, this life flowing in you. If you're near someone you can touch right now, reach out and take their wrist. Look at how fragile it is, how easy it would be to open a vein and wound them—or fill them.

Jesus's blood says: Because I love you and I don't want you to be afraid, I have gone ahead of you into everything bad that can and will happen to you. I have gotten there first. Look for me when you get there. I will have a cup, a cannula, communion, ready for you.

One reason we have to take communion over and over again is because once is not enough. The world can be one long chemo session that leaches life from our veins, and we all need to be restored from time to time. My first blood transfusion that Saturday was good—and also not enough. By Sunday, I didn't feel well, but went to church anyhow. At coffee hour, I stayed in my lawn chair outside after the Blessing of the Animals worship. People brought their coffee cups to me and sat around my feet like great skirts of humanity. It was embarrassing and sweet. They just wanted to huddle and buffer me against the world.

Monday, I pretended to feel better, calling on some of my old hustle. I drove Rafe to orchestra camp, and Carmen and I washed the car, and I did three loads of laundry, and took the kids to the park, in the beautiful sunny sun, when the not-feeling-so-good resolved itself into a newfangled fever, body aches, and chills. My temp went up to 103. By the time Peter got home, I was packed and ready for the hospital.

I went bald to the ER at the Brigham, crying and holding Peter's waist. (Hint: if ever you have to go to the ER, go bald, in your pajamas, crying, and holding somebody around the waist. You'll get right to the top of the waiting list.)

They tested my blood and told me I was neutropenic, my white blood cell count dangerously low. Infusions can only replace red blood cells, not white. My immune system was helpless against the marauding hordes of bacteria that stalk the earth. I would have to isolate until my counts recovered naturally. Even at the top of the list, it took six hours to get admitted, and another two before they would leave me alone to sleep.

I cried with madness and sadness and scaredness. I was off schedule. I was supposed to get through chemo in twenty-eight weeks. I had only made it through seven before I hit a wall. I'd never gone into the hospital as a sick person, just as an expectant mother, or a perfectly healthy person having a lung tumor taken out. This setback meant giving up my "off" week, which I had packed to the hilt with doctor-prescribed fun, healing, and exercise.

But God works by subtraction as well as addition, I reminded myself in the sadness and scaredness. Sometimes, God pares back the layers of our life, down to blood and bones, to see what really matters. I was about to find out.

Chapter 5

OUT OF THE MOUTHS OF BABES

The psalmist says, "Out of the mouths of babes and infants you have founded a stronghold because of your foes, to silence the enemy."

We love to quote just the start of that verse as a punchline whenever the kids in our lives say something cute. But the psalm is actually communicating something much more powerful: kids are truthtellers. Just ask one what they *really* think of your new haircut or your breath.

Kids are closer to the Source than we are, uncorrupted by the accretion of ego, power, and money. It hasn't been so long since they left wherever we come from before we are Here, and for this reason, they are more spiritually tuned in and connected to the divine. (Particularly at age four! What is it about four-year-olds and their terrifying spiritual questions?)

A friend of mine, newly a mother, once quipped, "Children ruin your life—for the better." We don't have to become parents for this ruining to happen. Lucky for us, kids are everywhere, especially if we plant ourselves in a church or another community where we regularly get to work and play with them.

When Peter and I had been dating for only six months, halfway through our last year in seminary, we decided to move to a foreign country together upon graduation and be poor on purpose. We figured if we could survive that so early on, we could survive anything.

No self-respecting religious setting I could find would accept an unmarried couple (we were audacious about the tensile strength of our young relationship, but not foolhardy enough to get hitched). The Casa San Jose in Colima, Mexico, was the only taker.

The Casa was an orphanage in a sweet city near the Pacific coast, home to about 140 children ages two through eighteen. Most of them did have some family, but were there because of either abuse/neglect or because their family was too poor to care for them. The Casa provided shelter, hot meals, health care, a public school on-site, and, when money and bandwidth were sufficient, art, computer, and choir.

Life at the Casa was organized chaos, partly because, Mexico, and partly because for most of its history, the Casa had a shadow government. Day-to-day operations happened under the direction of the benevolent dictator Lupita Muñiz and her staff of capable Mexican social workers. But an American priest, Father Francis Welsmiller (a.k.a. The Padre), whose family money had founded the Casa, still held the purse strings and ran the adjunct American volunteer program.

Mostly what The Padre actually did was experiment with soybean crops, hoping to find a cheap, protein-rich milk substitute for the kids. He deputized Joyce, a chain-smoking, wild-eyed, retired Floridian with manic tendencies to review volunteer applications and invite starry-eyed young Americans, some with white-savior complexes and others with even more suspect motives, to come live at the Casa for a year for room and board and one hundred dollars a month. Once there, they would do whatever work they could scrabble together without any real direction.

The volunteers with a white-savior complex were one problem; the others were another. There was the Arizonan who didn't do any work and was fond of inviting prostitutes to his bedroom. There was the Texan plumber who was dying of throat cancer and thought he would find himself a nice young Mexican wife to take care of him in his decline (at least he did some actual plumbing). And there was a host of other young people just like us, of varying levels of skill, effectiveness, and work ethic, including Tony, who didn't speak a word of Spanish and whom we overheard one day in downtown Colima ordering "un slice-o de pizza."

Soon after our first kissing-versary, Peter and I drove three thousand miles in our old jalopy to Colima. When we showed up on a blisteringly hot September day, Joyce had to be woken up from her siesta to welcome us. "I didn't know you were coming!" she said. She didn't mean that day. She meant at all.

Being unmarried, we had separate bedrooms at opposite ends of the compound. Giant tumbleweeds of drying soybeans needed to be cleared from Peter's room above Padre's lair. My room was empty, apart from the giant palmetto bugs who were my constant companions.

As the newest arrivals to the Casa, we were enormously interesting to the kids, who all promptly abandoned what they were doing—the daily Sisyphean task of sweeping the dirt, playing with the stray dogs, or trying to resurrect a deflated basketball—to help us unpack and show us around.

Yuridia, a seven-year-old with dimples so big I had to be careful not to fall into them, promptly took my hand and declared herself my person. I would later find out that she had three other siblings at the Casa and a sweet and cognitively impaired mother. Yuridia and the many other kids did everything they could to make us feel at home.

But that night, after cleaning my room and laying out my few things, the steel door clanged shut, and I was alone, for the first time in a long time.

The early weeks were hectic as we struggled to communicate in our newly adopted language and build out some infrastructure so that we could actually do something useful. Peter was preparing to teach computer technology, while I was charged by Padre with instilling in the children a deep and abiding love of Jesus. But the keys to the locked, abandoned classrooms had gone missing, the elementary-age children I was to teach were mostly illiterate, and no one with any know-how had time to help us figure things out because they had their own jobs to do.

Little by little, we built our programs. The first few weeks were exhilarating: the kids were thrilled to have new people to interrupt the sameness of their days. I decided to teach my students to read before diving into their spiritual education, which made sense since reading always rivaled Jesus as my first God. I had no training in any kind of pedagogy nor classroom management skills, but I had overweening self-confidence.

After school, Peter played soccer with the kids on the cement *cancha*, and I would play Uno, or read to them from the few Spanish books I had brought. I fell into bed every night exhausted, covered in a quarter-inch layer of kid dirt, too tired to brave the unlit bathroom and the *animalitos* that lurked within.

Next, Peter and I set about to organize the American volunteers, believing we would magically transform from a ragtag group of rivals into a high-powered team, just like in the movies.

Our efforts to be *that* scene in movies where chaos becomes order and natural divisions are overcome by grace, grit, and goodwill fell flat. We irritated some of the volunteers. And alarmed the social workers. What was happening? The Mexican staff was content with ineffectual Americans not meddling with their MO. It looked like we were going to ruin everything.

As a kid growing up on food stamps who had clawed her way into some lofty places (setting aside for a moment the whiteness that had also fueled my ascent), the guide ropes that kept me from falling were: work hard, be as smart and organized as you can, get shit done, and outrun all the monsters. None of these strategies applied in Mexico in general and at the Casa specifically, which didn't appreciate my can-do spirit and zeal for reform.

I spent one naive and idealistic night offering respite care for the toddler housemothers when four-year-old twins with fetal-alcohol-syndrome smeared poop on the walls with their flip-flops while singing at the top of their lungs. Their arias woke up the other thirty-four children who had various forms of trauma and fear of the dark. It was pandemonium and ended in tears. Mine.

Half the students in my literacy class were always MIA; I'd spend the first twenty minutes hunting the Casa grounds for them. It turns out three years of systematic theology does not prepare you for teaching in a Mexican classroom, even if you've read Paulo Freire's *Pedagogy of the Oppressed*. Even the kids who showed up regularly showed no sign of actually learning how to read. Not even Yuridia, who never missed a class and seemed to ascribe to the notion I had shared for so long: education could be a portal to something better.

The workaholic self I had carefully constructed to make myself a valued and therefore indispensable person wherever I went found no purchase. I was exhausted from trying to speak Spanish all day. I was also homesick for my family and friends. And my shoes were constantly filled with giant cockroaches luxuriating in their four-star accommodations.

Apart from the aforementioned intense but short-lived bouts of emo during my teenage years, I had never struggled with depression. But now I found there were days when I couldn't get out of bed, glued there by an insufferable weight and a grim haze. Peter would try to jolly me up and out the door, and when I resisted, gave up and gently tucked me in, then went and taught my kids alongside his. I cried myself to sleep after we had to say goodnight and go to our separate rooms. I was lonely, and even the nights when I found the courage to sneak over to Peter's bedroom for a cuddle were haunted by knowing it would end well before sunup because The Padre, downstairs, was an early riser.

It so happened that Henri Nouwen's *Gracias!* was one of the few books I had brought with me on our cross-country trek: an account of his travels as a priest through Peru and Bolivia, during which he became cripplingly depressed. He writes,

> At home we at least had our own niche in life, our own place in the world where we could feel useful and admired. Here none of that is present. Here we are in a world that did not invite us, in which we cannot express ourselves and which constantly reminds us of our powerlessness. And still, we know that we are sent here, that God wants us here, and that it is here that we have to work out our salvation.

I wanted nothing more than to get in my jalopy and drive home to Boston, if my ancient car would carry me all the way back, but I had never quit anything in my life and I couldn't bring myself to start now. I begged Peter to marry me so we could at least be together every night, but he wisely told me that was not a solution. I would have to work out my own salvation, with fear and trembling.

Through the haze of depression, and the fear of having my sunny, busy, false self stripped from me, I knew I had to learn a different way of living. A way that would accept that I am loved not for what I do, but simply for who I am. (A way I am still learning, frankly, many years into my practice of recovery from workaholism.)

But it turns out, I didn't have to go far for healing. The children, if I hadn't appeared by noon, would come calling through the metal bars of the glassless window of my room. I would crunch into a fetal position on my bed, just out of view of the window so they couldn't see my feet. They would disappear, only to reappear holding avocados and limes, which they knew I loved, harvested from trees in the Casa courtyard. They would toss them through the window, some of them turning instantly into guacamole from the fall. They would practice the English words I had taught them, most commonly calling for "BA-NA-NA! Ba-na-na please! I'm a MON-KEE!" when they spied fruit on top of my rusty refrigerator.

Sometimes, I waited them out, depression overwhelming my natural extraversion. Other times, I found the wherewithal to drag myself from the bed, push bananas through the window as if I were a zoo animal feeding the tourists, and thus free myself from the cage. From there, I only had to creep as far as the stairs outside my bedroom and sit. The kids would cluster around me, braid my hair, sing silly songs, demanding nothing but my relatively larger adult presence, unmoving, unleaving, something precious few of them had known in their lives.

The source of my pain became my medicine. As the children sought me out and sat with me, I healed.

(Important note: It is not the job of the children in our lives to heal us. Some of us in here grew up parentified, feeling responsible for our mothers' and fathers' feelings, or worse, actually being responsible for their well-being.)

Invited instead to play with the children rather than labor for them, I began to unlearn habits of workaholism at the Casa. Over time, when I neither abandoned the enterprise nor sought to take it over, the Mexican staff grew to trust and love me and I them. I am blessed to call Lupita, the director, a spiritual sister to this day. Lupita and I, both functional firstborns from dysfunctional families, remind each other that it doesn't all depend upon us—and that as much as we want to do right by God, God doesn't put all Her eggs in the basket of one leader.

One useful thing I learned in seminary to apply to this moment came from my pastoral care professor. She taught us the phrase "ministry of presence," which to a do-er like me, sounded like bullshit. But it's what Yuridia, and Toñito, and Claudia, and many others did for me. They hadn't demanded anything of me (other than a few bananas). They hadn't offered me advice, or tried to fix me, or made their love conditional in any way. They just kept showing up.

To some degree, I saw myself in those kids. They who loved their alcoholic, abusive, neglectful, or mentally ill parents, who arbitrarily showed up on a Sunday afternoon to take them out for *un paseo* only to leave them weeping, returned back to the monotony of institutional life on Sunday evening. Maybe the depression was something deferred from my own childhood to now, when I had the adulthood and agency to experience it, to find the edges and limits of it. And with it, to face that there was only so much I could do for those kids. I, too, was passing through for only a short *paseo*. As it turns out, I was nobody's savior.

I began to understand that I had choices. I could decide not to get in my jalopy and be one more person leaving. At least for now.

We ended up staying for thirteen months before deciding it was time to go home and see our families and start the next chapter of our lives. About five months in, my students had made enough progress in reading that I rewarded them with a walking field trip to the ice cream shop a few blocks away. Yuridia, bursting with pride, read every single sign along the way, a tour guide for the others, and when we arrived at the *heladeria*, she helped them navigate the thirty-nine flavors, from *elote* to *sardinas en tomate*.

On our last day, the following September, Yuri put into my hand a drawing: Peter, me, and herself in front of a house with flowerbeds in front. The jalopy long ago junked, we climbed onto the second-class bus, and I held that picture, crying through the next three states.

All those kids, now grown, I see on Facebook. Some have made it over the border, making a life for themselves here in the United States or elsewhere. Some have gone on to university or come out of the closet and into their own glory. Many are raising their own kids, the families they craved back then. Yuri is a registered nurse with two beautiful little girls. And she is still in school, bettering herself.

Of course, I'm seeing filtered front stages that mask a lot of suffering, poverty, and tragedy. But whenever an old photo of our year together surfaces on our feeds, these "kids" who have so few visual records of their past say things to each other like, "Those really were the best times. We had so much fun together. Childhood is a blessing." When I read those notes, I believe they really mean it.

When Jesus called the little children to him, it wasn't some kind of sentimental photo op. He was both drawing on their holy energy and offering them some of his. It was a moment of undiluted communion and mutual enjoyment.

By bathing ourselves in children's natural light and joy and wonder and curiosity and need, we discover their babblings are often a telegram from God, one able to drown out the noise of our worst enemies fear, insecurity, depression, anxiety, pettiness, jealousy, and judgment.

The lessons I learned from the kids at the Casa continued to follow me. Long after we returned and early in my cancer journey, after surgery and before chemo, two of our church kids in particular gave me the courage and perspective I needed to go on.

Eight-year-old George was a wild redhead like me, but came by his hair naturally. He was given to bow ties and serious conversations about philosophy and engineering.

One thing I loved about George was how comfortable he was with adults. Not shy the way lots of kids are nor especially gregarious, playing for attention, but just—an equal. We were both at a barbecue at bestie Sue and Jason's house just before I started chemo. I had been feeling pretty normal and good, chatting about weather and vacations, then the conversational winds shifted to other people. I was quiet, watching this party, watching people in their delicious normalcy, suddenly realizing how much everything was going to change for me while it stayed more or less the same for everybody else. It was a dissonant, lonely feeling.

George ambled up to me where I was sitting on the stoop and plunked himself down, warm and leaning in. He looked up at me with the most pastoral expression and said, "How did your surgery go?"

"It went great. Don't I look great?"

He nodded cheerfully. "Yeah, you really do!"

"My incisions are really small—the surgeon did a very good job."

"My classmate has a brain tumor," he announced. I asked if she was bald. "Yes! But it's just side effects from her medicine," he reassured me. "Her medicine kills fast-growing cells because cancer is a fast-growing cell, but so is hair."

"I'm going to lose my hair, too," I told him. Then we talked about fingernails for a while—how they are made of hair, but don't fall out with chemo. We were both curious about that, so he said he would look into that for me. Then we just sat there, in peace. I was so glad to have this small, solid someone to hold my hand as I stood there, at the end of the diving board, looking down.

A couple of weeks later, in church, I was chatting with Luke, who was six. I'd known Luke since a few weeks after he was born. I remember the day he came into church in the sling with his mom, Ellen, and his dad, Eric. Luke had gone to Rafe and Carmen's daycare, so over the years, we'd had a lot of good chats during the daycare carpool. He had a round-eyed sweetness and natural warmth.

We hadn't been as close in the years since he aged out of our carpool, but I was tickled when he came right up to me at coffee hour and said, "At school, they told us about this bike ride for kids, to raise money to help people who have cancer. And I said to myself, 'Molly's having some cancer! I could do that.'"

It somehow cut down to size the vast, monolithic power of cancer. It's not Cancer. It's, you know, *some* cancer. There's choice implied, and moderation. Like going to tea at The Ritz, "I'll have a scone, a little prosecco, some cancer, please—I'm watching my figure."

The next week, Ellen took Luke and Rafe on the Pan-Mass Challenge Kids' Ride in Concord to raise money for Dana Farber, my cancer treatment center. Ellen is a child psychologist and thought it might help Rafe gain some mastery over his worry to have a way to contribute at a time like this, because eight-year-old Rafe, while quiet since we had told our kids the cancer news, had clearly been worried.

I'm normally very open with my kids. But we didn't tell Rafe or Carmen about the specter of cancer during the long process of surgery and biopsy because: why worry them if it wasn't necessary?

Before we had children, I knew the mother I wanted to be—relaxed, fun, always doing messy crafts, playing endless loops of Fairy Club or Thomas the Train Time. That is, the opposite of the mother who raised me. And yes, I am a fun mom, loving and creative, but also impatient, a neatnik, a too-frequent yeller, and when we were both younger, frighteningly fierce with my very strong-willed son.

Rafe was a tricky kid. If I was too easygoing, he'd charm the socks off of me to everyone's disadvantage, including his own; if I was too hard on him, he'd rebel against authority and ultimately against his own self-interest.

Then I got sick. And, having made a choice, in that dream, to stay here on Earth, I had a new vision of the mother I longed to be if I got to live. When I finally told my kids about my cancer diagnosis, it revealed their personalities and temperaments to me like nothing else. Eight-year-old Rafe countered with a desperate bravado trying to wall himself off from pain. Four-year-old Carmen, ever the pleaser and caretaker, danced faster, smiled harder, trying to distract us from the pain.

The day after we learned of the diagnosis, we sat them down on our bed. "You know how I went into the hospital and they took a ball out of my lung? Well, they looked at it really, really closely, and they finally decided that it is cancer. Cancer is when some cells in the body start to grow really fast, and sometimes when they grow so fast, they make it hard for the body to do its jobs." I told them about the process, that I'd be given strong medicine, and it would help, but I'd be really tired. When I got to telling them, "It will make all my hair fall out," Carmen, at this point, laughed out loud—angling for comic relief.

I went on, "It's important to remember that all the ways I might feel bad are *not* because of the cancer, but because of the strong medicine. That seems silly, but that's the way it works."

That was it, more or less. The children nodded gravely and we talked a bit more about when my hair would fall out, how other people would be taking them on playdates, or picking them up from school because of my chemo schedule. We told them if they had any questions they wanted to ask, any funny feelings to talk about, they could ask us anything. And if they didn't feel like asking us, they could find another adult they felt close to talk about it with. "Who are some adults you feel close to?"

"Sue, Jason, Leslie, Sam, Kerrie, Andrea," they said, naming a long list of loving adults in our life and church. "Althea, Jen Brown…" They were clearly covered in that department. And then they were done—ready to move on and go back to playing. We followed their cues and let them go.

They didn't ask if I was going to die. I wasn't fooled. I duly noted the absence of the question. Rafe had been obsessed with death since he was two, and there was no way the omission was accidental. But kids process things in their own way, at their own pace.

A couple of days later, it finally came, but not as a question. Rafe woke up very early in the morning, came to our bedroom door, and said simply, "I need comfort." Peter comforted. It turns out he'd been reading *The Lightning Thief*—the mother gets killed off early in the book. Fuck. Did I need to pre-screen everything these days?

Later that afternoon, we were lolling about on the couch. If your family is ever facing huge challenging times, be sure to do a lot of extra lolling. Not only is it fun and relaxing but it also gives your children a chance to talk to you in an indirect way about what is happening.

Rafe said, "I needed comfort last night because I was reading that book, and then I fell asleep and dreamed that you died."

"That must have been scary," I said.

"It was," he said. "You know how, when I was little and I asked about death, and I'd say I didn't want you and Dad to die, you'd say you were most probably going to live to be old? You said that a lot of things had to happen before you would die, like I would become a teenager, then go to college, then fall in love and get married, then have my own children, then have different jobs, then get a little bit old myself and maybe stop working, and maybe I'd even become a grandfather?"

"Yes," I said.

"Well, you might not. You have cancer. You might just live a short time."

"You're right about that."

"Sometimes, I think you are going to live a long time, and other times, I think you are going to die, and other times, I just don't know."

I said, quietly, "That's about where I am."

I have never lied to my kids, mostly because I am a terrible liar, but also because I think kids, even young kids, deserve the truth.

And they need the truth at their own pace, which means not burdening them with more information than they have sought or answers to questions they haven't asked. But I also believe that kids notice more than we think they do. Especially my kids—when Rafe was little, he wouldn't hear the nine times I asked him to put on his shoes, but if I was two rooms away whispering to a friend about his latest tantrum, I would suddenly hear from the living room a shrill "I heard that! How dare you!"

Knowing that kids hear and know more than we imagine, and that they are more resilient than we give them credit for, I felt it was important to start preparing them for death early—as the most natural, holy thing, and deeply a part of life.

So, on this particular day, I told Rafe the truth: most of the time, I thought I was going to live a long, long time. Then I took him by the shoulders and brought him over to the computer. I showed him the 153 kind comments on my Facebook post from friends after disclosing my diagnosis. I showed him the vast list of emails with prayers embedded in them. Together, we counted the number of clergy who said their communities of faith were praying for me. We did the math. I didn't tell him what to think or feel, but I asked him, "What do you think about that?"

He thought, but didn't say anything.

Carmen took a couple of extra days to get around to the question. Being four at the time, she was very concrete and all about assuring her own security. About a year earlier, she had developed a line of questioning to make certain that I would never abandon her. "Will you still be my mom when I am a grown woman? Will you still be my mom when I am a mom? Will you still be my mom when I am crabby, or when I cry, or when I hit?" There were many variations on this theme. I assured her that I would always be her mom, no matter what, no matter when.

Then, a week after the diagnosis, there was a new iteration. We were driving to daycare, making our way slowly up Broadway.

"Will you still be my mom when I am a teenager?" she asked.

"Yup, Carm, I will be your mom when you are a teenager. You may wish I weren't, then," I said archly.

Then, casually, she asked, "Will you still be my mom when you are in heaven?"

Thunk went my heart.

"Yes, Carm, I will be your mom even when I'm in heaven," I answered evenly, trying to match her mood.

A street sweeper cut off our progress across Teele Square. "Hey, Mom, what's that?" She had already moved on, with typical four-year-old in-the-momentness. I, meanwhile, managed to hold it together until I dropped her off. But eight blocks later, I was crying so hard that when I stopped at a red light, a kind man in the Porsche in front of me got out of his car and asked me if I was all right.

The thing about having young kids while in cancer treatment is that the poignancy was almost too much at times—the terrible daymares about dying and Carmen having only the vaguest of memories about me, the wondering if Rafe would always feel cheated and a little bit bereft, suppressed grief giving way to self-sabotage. At the same time, I was intensely grateful for the dozens of ways every day that having young children forced me to stay in the present, grounded and enfleshed.

I didn't have the luxury of going off into the stratosphere, ruminating all day long about death. There were still permission slips to sign, lunches to pack, dinner to fix, homework to check, bottoms to wipe, asthma medicine to puff, stories to read, and nightmares to suck out of ears (our family's standard operating procedure).

Even on those nights when Peter, or his mother, Sarah, or my dad, George, entirely took over the childcare tasks while I took to bed chemo-addled, the kids would sneak off and find me. They wouldn't ask, at four and eight, "So, how are your thoughts of mortality today?" They wanted to play I Spy, or have a ticklefest, or talk about how the class clown got them in trouble (Rafe) or recount their growing pains (Carm).

Every morning, they made me start the day with a dance party. Anything by ABBA and Michael Franti's "Say Hey" were crowd favorites. My sweet children made me happy every day, and probably, over the course of ten months of chemo, built more white blood cells than the Neulasta shots I gave myself.

Still, as the bruises on my arms grew from being stuck with needles so many times, the biggest bruise was this: imagining that my children would be orphaned, scarred for life by losing me too soon, or perhaps worse—forgetting me entirely. And I'd miss so much.

When I broke down crying at my desk one day, God spoke to me again and told me in no uncertain terms that, whether I lived or died, my children would be all right. "Wounded and shaped for life by this experience, but all right. You and Peter have built for them a very strong container in the form of a large and loving circle of friends, family, and chosen family. If you die, they have angels in abundance who will help them heal and transform their grief, someday, into strength."

A simple "You will survive," would have done, God.

But God doesn't answer prayers with that kind of certainty. God tells us what we need to hear, not what we want to hear. That's how we know it's God, a better parent than many of us have had. And there is a strange sort of comfort in God's tough love, reminding us that the world, even our children's, doesn't entirely revolve around nor depend upon us.

Chapter 6

THE HOLY SPIRIT PORTAL

In my early cancer days, a friend gave me a tiny silver bird necklace. Instead of a chain, it came on a thread. The instructions on the paper card that came with it said to make a wish when I put it on. When the necklace broke, my wish would come true.

I wasn't ready to put it on when I got it because I knew it wouldn't last until my chemo ended about ten months later. And my wish was, in some sort of inchoate way, something about the end of chemo.

When I finally put it on, it nestled up against the "Heal" necklace my sister-in-law Tia Carmen gave me when I was first diagnosed. Together, they felt like a talisman against dark forces. But I never really came to clarity about what my wish was.

I left the wish unformed because if I put the thought into it to make an airtight wish, a wish that whatever amoral bureaucratic genie who governs wishes could not find a loophole in, I would not have any thought leftover for really necessary tasks, like "Look in rearview mirror while backing out of steep, icy driveway into traffic," or "Wash hands *after* wiping child's bottom and *before* putting cookie in mouth."

Prayers, on the other hand, don't require so much anxiety or specificity. Over time, I learned to pray about my cancer, out of either laziness or surrender, with this one prayer: God, thy will be done.

I became comfortable praying that prayer because I was by then pretty sure that God was not an asshole. Most of the time, I remain pretty sure about this. I am not going just on faith but also on empirical evidence. There is not one 'bad' thing that has happened to me in my life that I have not seen the good hand of God at work within. My prayer is a common-sense prayer, as I see it. A partnership prayer. I don't have to over-think and put myself in knots of anxiety about what to pray. I just have to live each day, and look for the hand of God.

This is how it is with the wish genie when you might have cancer: you make a wish and hope the string doesn't break, really, ever, because then you're in an either-or situation. Your wish will either have come true, or it won't.

This is how it is with God when you have cancer: one week, the exhaust system on your car blows and you have five days of chemo in a row. The next week, a massage therapist friend shows up on your doorstep with empty hands, full of grace. Anonymous sweeties leave cookies for your children on your porch without ringing the doorbell, fleeing into the darkness as you try to holler thanks after them. And you get a call from the minister who confirmed you as a teenager, his elderly voice halting but strong on your voicemail, to tell you that he did indeed hold a baby yesterday, just as the Advent calendar you sent him suggested, and the baby yawned.

Are we silver birds on a thread that threatens to break any minute? If we were indeed as precious as silver and gold, would God keep us on a cotton thread? Matthew's gospel says, "Are not two sparrows sold for a penny? Yet not one of them will fall to the ground apart from the will of your Abba God."

In modern parlance: God actually gives a shit about us. But God is not a wish genie. And prayer is neither wish-fulfillment nor putting God to the test. Prayer is a way of finding out what we really want, opening our hearts to whatever will come, our worst fears and best hopes, our projections and reality-checks, and getting gradually free of fear.

The people in my church circles are, for the most part, not better at prayer than you. Even if they have been keeping a pew warm for fifty years, they struggle to find the words, the time, the motivation. They've heard roughly 1.7 million sermons on prayer, and still, they and I forget that prayer can be as simple as saying, "Are you there, God? It's me," then leaving God room to say something back, however God gets through. "Mental prayer," wrote the contemplative nun and doctor of the church, Teresa of Ávila, "is simply a friendly [and] frequent solitary conversation with [God] who, as we know, loves us."

Of course, humans have found a way to complicate prayer, as we have everything else. Even me, a professional pray-er. Some of the toggles on the switchboard of prayer that continue to confound me are: When I tell someone I will pray for them, how often should I pray? Do I need to use words, or is thinking of them enough, or is simply *breathing* for them enough? What if they are praying to get stinking rich, or for their mortal enemy to have a painless but debilitating stroke, or for a pet unicorn? Can I change the prayer to be a little more ethical or based in reality?

Most importantly: when does the promise-to-pray end? When their situation is entirely resolved? Which likely means: when they are dead? This seems a little unworkable, as I inherit more and more prayers. When would I do the laundry?

There is also the question of what is happening spiritually when you agree to pray for someone. Am I a vessel for prayers—prayers that then get lodged in me permanently, spiritual sludge? Or am I a channel for prayer, a human operator with a thick Jersey accent running wires between God and other humans? Am I loudspeaker, the "human microphone" developed for activists during the low-tech Occupy movement, repeating the longings of one human at volume, hoping to catch God's ear? If so, does that mean more people praying is better?

And the ten-dollar question: whether praying for ourselves, others, or the world in general, if God knows everything, why bother praying? If God is omniscient, God already knows. And if God is omnipotent, God would have done something about it already. And if God hasn't, is God really an asshole after all?

A few years ago, three dear friends, a married couple and their adult daughter, were driving home from a week of running a high-school musical at my church camp when they were hit head-on. The driver of the other car, sick on opioids, got distracted at the wheel and his SUV jumped the median. Ledell and Kat, her beautiful daughter, succumbed to their injuries. Don, though he was the most battered of the three with thirty-eight broken bones and a traumatic brain injury, lived on in a coma for almost a month. We sensed that he was trying to stay alive for their twenty-eight-year-old son, Devan, who had ridden home from camp with friends. If Don died, Devan would be alone.

Every day we sang to Don, in person and over the phone. He had a community of thousands—fellow musicians, students and friends, including many serious Christians—praying for him daily for a month. But in the end, his body was too wrecked. The tragedy of losing the Mulvaneys so senselessly, on their way home from a week at effing church camp volunteering with teenagers, made us all confront the idea of prayer's efficacy and the nature of God. Could God possibly be THAT much of an asshole?

Superstitious tendencies or mental illness can muddle our minds and send us down another rabbit hole of wrecked thinking about prayer. Like: God not only let Jesus—a really good guy—and maybe even His Own Son, die by slow, painful violence. He also let an entire Christian industry be built and profit off the idea that it was all intentional.

My church gets a lot of refugees from other corners of Christianity, people who are decolonizing their faith from fundamentalism, and some of that stinkin' thinking persists. I basically feel like my job in this situation is to say, as many times as necessary, "God loves you, enormously. God doesn't want to punish you. God doesn't require you to be any different from who you are. God is looking out for your highest good, and no, I don't think God can prevent bad things from happening to you, but God will not abandon you in your distress and fear, and God will weep with you when you are weeping, and God will send angels both human and divine to help you out of the tight spots, and God will strengthen you for whatever you have to face."

I've pastored a woman with bipolar disorder that is generally well-managed, but when her brain goes a little haywire, she hears voices. That is when she needs reminding that God loves her, that she is not an agent of evil, that God wants her to stay alive, talk to her psychiatrist, take her medication, and have the occasional hospitalization when things really go out of control.

I've pastored a young gay international student from an authoritarian, antigay country who has struggled with OCD since he was young. The social distancing rules governing the pandemic exacerbated his OCD and his growing faith gave it a religious cast. Together with a short run of bad luck relating to his immigration status and intense pressure at school, it put him in a fragile mental and spiritual state, afraid he would lose God's support and be punished if he didn't do everything exactly "right." Was he praying "correctly"? Was he certain enough in his faith? If he accidentally gave his roommates COVID, was that not only a violation of the command to love one's neighbor—was it, in fact, murder?

He needed kind human voices to remind him of God's kindness—his pastors and his mental health companion from church. At one point, he sent me an email. "God said to me that it is good that I worked hard to seek Him, but I don't need to be this fearful, I can relax. That I suffer for being so fearful." He wrote more about the God-exchange he had, and he ended it, "God paused, and said firmly, 'It will get better.'"

When the cancer diagnosis first came in, one of my church ladies, Debbie, gave me a resin tchotchke that said, "Prayer changes things." I put it on the shelf above my desk. On my more scared and cynical days, I'd yell at it. "Oh really? Did it change things for Jesus, crying in the garden of Gethsemane, asking God to take this cup from him the night before he went to *his* death?"

But about 79 percent of the time, I manage to believe it. I don't think of prayer as magic, or a panacea, but an assist. When you're a novice rock climber, all you see from below is the impossibility of ascent. Beginners need the biggest handholds, and use the smallest muscles, trying to pull themselves up with puny biceps and triceps. You have to use the bigger muscles, glutes and quads, to push yourself up, a rock-climbing instructor will tell you, rather than the smaller muscles. From below, they'll also shout to offer the more nuanced handholds they can see, holds invisible to you because of your inexperience, fear, and myopia.

Having a regular practice of prayer is rock climbing. Instinct and culture tell us to use small muscles to try to lift ourselves up: ego, ambition, substances, overwork. But prayer trains us to use the big muscles. One of the largest muscles is gratitude—when exercised, it can lift us up almost effortlessly. Another big muscle is orientation to others in prayer: their needs, their hurts, the pain of the wider world, putting our own in perspective.

A sustained practice of prayer reveals to us all the smaller handholds we missed when we were beginners: the varying paths available to us on the ascent. God, the spotter below, with a firm hold on the belay line, can't prevent you from falling, but She is shouting up to you the handholds you can't see, and She is there to keep you from plummeting to your death.

As with anything, we might let the fact that we are beginners, with our puny biceps, put us off from even starting. Why not just stay on the sofa, spiritually speaking? Because whatever else prayer changes, it definitely changes *us*. So, begin anywhere. After I ask my people, "Have you prayed about it?" and get their embarrassed, "No, not really," responses, I tell them, "Start with a 'selfish' prayer, not a noble one. Pray very specifically for what you really want. Pray for the stage 4 tumor to magically dry up. Pray for your child to sober up. Pray for the suicidal depression to lift. Even starting the conversation is creating an opening for *something* to change."

Not everybody gets a happy ending. But prayer can make the right-now more bearable. As I write this, we are still living through the pandemic. Some of my people are living a grueling Groundhog Day, working intense jobs from home while caring for disabled partners and small children, handicapped by a chronic depression or anxiety that the virus has turned the volume all the way up on. But praying as they can helps them take a longer view and create new neural footholds that at least sometimes help reroute their perseverating minds. They can pray gratitude for the slobber-kisses of toddlers and modern science delivering vaccines at warp speed. However hard any individual day is, they can pray, like Jesus, to let this cup pass from them and, like Jesus, look for resurrection, eventually.

Devan, six years after the death of his parents and sister, wrote recently, "I've been experiencing hope and joy the past few months that I haven't felt in years. Through a lot of self-work, I've realized that over the past years I've struggled with survivor's guilt. It's kept me from fully living in the moment and it's prevented me from taking joy in wholeheartedly when it comes my way. I've often felt that the best years of my life, the ones where my family was still alive, are behind me. This is the guilt talking. I'm starting to finally open myself up to the idea that it's very possible that I can have incredible moments, dare I say the best moments I've ever had, without my family and that I shouldn't feel guilty for that, that it's something they would want me to have. Because of my loss, I've grown a new hyperawareness for seeing and appreciating joyful moments and knowing which life struggles are truly worthy of my frustration or sadness…It's a remarkable aspect of going through something difficult, that you have this new way of looking at the world that you didn't have before."

Prayer is a way of feeling everything. As Rainer Maria Rilke said, "Let everything happen to you, beauty and terror. Just keep going. No feeling is final." If we can have our feelings, they won't have us in some occult and ultimately more pernicious way.

Not wanting to burden God with our prayers is like not wanting to burden a tree with our carbon dioxide. Prayer is a natural energy exchange between us and God, and God, like an empty nester, loves it when we call. We don't ever need to use *God* as the excuse for not praying.

During the pandemic, my church's business manager, who is a bonus minister of our church, found herself called in for jury duty. Kit doesn't drive and would have to take public transportation an hour in either direction if she were picked. Not to mention, who would do her job if she were empaneled?

I told her she should just loudly proclaim her Christian faith to the prosecutors, and that would probably take care of that. Whether it was that, or her purple hair, or the fact that she lived in Berzerkley, she was not picked.

When I saw her the next day, she said, "I started out praying not to get picked, but then my prayer morphed into a 'thy will be done' prayer. And it was crazy how it all worked out. I was released, and when I was dreading the ride home on BART, in the elevator with a two-person-per-ride limit, I discovered that the only other person in there with me was a woman who lived in Berkeley who had already been vaccinated. And she offered me a ride home." We agreed that there is something elegant about praying a "surrender prayer" to what will be. Somehow, our surrender is the key that often unlocks the cage we are in, and lets God, who has wanted our ease all along, better meet our desires, as long as they do no harm to others.

(That said, on the many occasions when God and I have a difference of opinion, I *still* believe God should reconsider. When we lived in Mexico, people would often respond, when talking about future events, "*Si Dios quiere,*" "*If* God wants it." I would usually respond, "*Sí, Dios quiere.*" "*Yes,* God wants it." What a difference a comma makes.)

The mystic and writer Simone Weil once said, "Attention, taken to its highest degree, is the same thing as prayer...Absolutely unmixed attention is prayer." Another way of saying this: whatever we pay attention to risks becoming our God. And in the "attention economy," even more agents are vying for our attention, monetizing that attention and leaving us fragmented and disoriented. We think we are using Facebook for connection, Twitter for news, Instagram for beauty, and a thousand other widgets on our tiny screens to get various jobs done, even as those minions of Satan are mining us for data, money, and more. We, in fact, are the widgets.

What if instead we harvested all that attention and with it powered prayer, in the Way of Simone Weil? Weil went on, "If we turn our mind toward the good, it is impossible that little by little the whole soul will not be attracted thereto in spite of itself." I know I sound like a granola mom imploring her children to eat 1,000 percent All Bran instead of Krunchy Kookie cereal. But

I know by now that more than a smidge of social media robs me of time and attention for my truest loves—absolutely unmixed attention to my family, friends, body, nature, and vocation—and leaves me feeling flattened out and anxious. Maybe you "social media" better than me and can game the system. Go you! But I have learned my limit.

To those who are still finding themselves apologists for your social media habits, read the artist, scholar, and amateur birder Jenny Odell's *How to Do Nothing: Resisting the Attention Economy.* "We experience the externalities of the attention economy in little drips, so we tend to describe them with words of mild bemusement like 'annoying' or 'distracting,'" she writes. "But this is a grave misreading of their nature. In the short term, distractions can keep us from doing the things we want to do. In the longer term, however, they can accumulate and keep us from living the lives we want to live, or, even worse, undermine our capacities for reflection and self-regulation, making it harder, in the words of Harry Frankfurt, to 'want what we want to want.' Thus, there are deep ethical implications lurking here for freedom, well-being, and even the integrity of the self."

As I was adjusting to the sudden pressure changes of early cancer adventures, I noticed an evolution in my reaction to difficult health news: hearty bravery, followed by slow panic, that sometimes metamorphosed into feeling unusually alive and grateful (all interspersed with angry outbursts at my safest people, usually my dad or Peter, or a noisy private crying jag).

Eventually, I would arrive back at a deeper brave again as the prayers of others took over. I felt every one of those hundreds, perhaps thousands, of prayers, nourishing the big muscles I would need for this climb. "Courage is fear that has said its prayers," as the silent film actress Dorothy Bernard said. More often than not, that courage is borrowed.

In my life as a pastor and a certified Christian™, I am often the one whose courage is called upon. When the world has gone mad, or just one person's world, I will find myself saying, "I will believe for you, until you can believe again. I will pray for you, until you can pray again."

For a long time, as strange as it sounds for a pastor, I was uncomfortable praying with people. I was worried I wouldn't find the right words, or that I would fumble a lot, or that I would get their prayers "wrong." I started saying "I'll pray for you," without regard for the fact that they might need someone to pray for them *right then*.

Over time, I've been able to take more of my own advice: to become okay with praying imperfectly, out loud, and immediately with others. I start with the selfish prayer, the small muscles. I remember to call on the big ones too, by way of assist—particularly, the big muscle of gratitude. "Thanks, God!" is a great opener.

When I'm out of words, I rest in a comma, or better yet, an ellipsis that leaves room for the person I'm praying with to fumble for their own words, spoken or silent. A quiet Amen seals the deal.

The first week after they found my tumor, I'm not sure God found me much of a conversation partner. My prayer was pretty much entirely "ohfuckohfuckohfuckohfuckohfuckohfuckohfuckohfuck FUCK ME."

Then the "selfish" prayers began to take shape. "Please let this CT scan reveal that it is an entirely benign growth that requires no further treatment and releases me back in time to finish my Easter sermon. And thanks for the great sermon illustration, God!" "Please let this second CT scan reveal (cut and paste from earlier prayer)."

Bestie Sue, who found time back in my cancer days to be my work wife at our church while also getting paid to be a physical therapist at Mt. Auburn Hospital in Cambridge, really believes in the power of God, *and* also really believes in modern medicine, what it can do to heal and cure.

THE HOLY SPIRIT PORTAL

This combination is harder to find than you might think, and it is absolutely essential in anyone applying to be your Best Friend Through Cancer Treatment.

In an email she sent as the news of the tumor was first landing on us, Sue said,

> *There is something evil about the suffering caused by illness, the injustice of it all, the opposition to life. There is also the idea that through our trauma there is a void that God can fill. God is there with us closely through it all. Simone Weil (whom I dig), wrote 'Grace (the blessing of God) fills empty spaces, but it can only enter where there is a void to receive it, and it is grace itself which makes this void.'*
>
> *This is another way of saying that we can't receive a gift if our hands are full. Are abnormal cells, cancers, viruses, bacterias, fears, addictions voids? Grace-given voids that allow us room to need and ask for something bigger than ourselves? That line of thinking can get pretty morbid and quickly so. What kind of God creates problems so that people will need God more?*
>
> *We are fearfully and wonderfully made. God grieves when we suffer. God blesses us with modern medicine and caring physicians because God wants us to be well when the natural order of the world opposes our health and comfort. And when we suffer, it is a chance for us to accept help, be befriended by Jesus, appreciate our complexities, our vulnerabilities and praise God for it all.*
>
> *xo*
> *Sue*

After my first scan, I met up with Sue in the hospital cafeteria for bad coffee. I still couldn't really believe I had cancer. I was flummoxed. "What could this be?" I asked her. "Maybe it's your Holy Spirit Portal," she said. A way for God to get in.

Later I was sitting behind a curtain in a wing of a Mt. Auburn Hospital bay, vulnerable in a johnny, when I heard the radiologist talking on the phone to the thoracic surgeon on call about the results of my CT scan.

"I still can't tell what this thing is—you want me to biopsy it, or do you want to just whack it out?"

Don't they know that sound can actually travel *through* polyester curtains, those doctors who think they are so smart?

He came in a few minutes later, flanked by three nurses whose legs were planted firmly on the linoleum, like the opening scene of some crime drama or spy show. Did they think I was going to make a break for it?

"The mass is still a mystery," he said. "We could biopsy it, but there's a risk of lung collapse, a subsequent hospital stay. And the biopsy might not even give us all the information we want. We all think you should have it taken out," the radiologist said.

When facing an unrepentant mansplainer with backup bouncer-nurses, I'm a bit of a contrarian.

"Doctor, can I ask you a personal question? Are you a person of faith?"

"What faith?" he asked, defensive.

"Any faith," I said.

"I'm Jewish," he said.

The nurses almost wet themselves at this point. Grilling docs about their faith is so *not done* in a Harvard-affiliated hospital.

"Do you pray?" I asked.

"No, not really," he said. "Why do you ask?"

"Well, I do pray, and it figures heavily into how I think about the world, how I make decisions. You are trained to see pathology in lots of places, so that's what you see. I'm trained to look for other things."

"Does that mean you won't have the surgery?"

"It means I want to pray about it."

What if God had given me this unique wireless device, a divine mobile communication, a portal to another dimension of living? And now I was just going to cut it out?

I met Sue for another cup of mediocre coffee and asked her what she thought I should do.

"If they think it's something possibly dangerous, you should let them take it out. Then you'll have an even bigger Holy Spirit Portal."

On the morning of surgery, Rafe and Carmen wrote love notes on my hands in Sharpie since I couldn't take anything into the operating room except for the body I arrived with. Carmen, age four, left her characteristic scribble on my left hand. Rafe, age eight, inscribed a heart with "We HEART Mom" and "Be Strong" on my right.

Everything else came off: wedding ring, nose ring, cross necklace. Surgery is one of those bizarre moments when we become unarmored and anonymized in the space of minutes. Robbed of our usual forms of self-definition: jewelry, clothing, and shoes are stuffed unceremoniously into a plastic sack. The nurse puts a Tyvek bracelet with your personal data on your wrist because once you are under anesthesia, you can't say who you are. You might be anybody. The next thing you know (except you don't because you have temporarily disappeared from your own life), you have been medicated to a point of suspended animation close to death, and strangers are putting their hands inside your body cavity and taking pieces out. When they're done, they wake you up. It's all very undignifying and strange.

After I woke up, nauseous and out of it and weeping with pain, I hollered for my husband.

"He can come in when you feel better," the nurses wheedled.

"I'll feel better when he comes in," I mustered right back. They gave in.

Peter gamely made his way to me through the post-op ward, past the crying and blood and smells that he later described as "A zombie apocalypse in miniature. A conveyor belt of reconstitution," to me, his zombie wife. He rubbed my feet and made little jokes, not enough to make me laugh and hurt even more, but enough to call me back into the light.

Afterward, they brought me to the ICU because there were no beds on the general postsurgical floors, and so, being young and basically healthy, they ignored me in favor of the dying people. I definitely felt like one of the dying people when the Dilaudid haze parted and I could feel everything a little too much. When they finally took out my chest tube, Peter took a look and said, "There's your stigmata," a perfectly round hole in my side. I breathed, and it sounded like someone was playing washboard on my ribs, or turning gears inside of me. My Holy Spirit Portal made music!

A few days later, they released me to go home, leaking from several stitched holes, the rusty machinery inside of me grinding to life again. Very often in those days, there was a part of me that was tired of being brave, and needed to sob, and regretted letting 40 percent of my lung go even though the alternative was certain death. Part of me stubbornly felt like surgery was the beginning of a long, long ending, where bits and pieces would gradually be taken out of my body and my soul and my family, and not replaced with anything equivalent or better.

One of my preaching heroes, Fred Craddock, said that a good sermon has a long beginning and a quick finish. A good life is the same. But for the weeks after surgery, I mostly felt like life had a quick start and a long ending.

Weeks later, the "envelope, please" moment of the pathology report finally arrived. Peter and I were summoned to meet with Dr. Butryinski, a sarcoma oncologist at Dana Farber Cancer Institute in Boston. He was a slight man with thinning brown hair, of middle height, a few years older than us, but with an ageless, kind, and bespectacled face.

It is a face I came to know very well over the next few years, but in that moment of meeting, his face was unreadable. He started slow, like Fred Craddock winding up for a sermon.

"We're going to take our time to talk through this, about the course this is going to take."

He didn't say "treatment options" or any other words that would have cued us immediately to the Big C, but told us my PET scan was clear. I snagged the happy word out of the air, landed it on my lap, and held it.

"It's clear—that's good, right?"

"Yes, but they've finished the pathology report, and finally identified this tumor as a Ewing's sarcoma—usually they're found in the bone. Very rare to find in soft tissue, even rarer in a lung."

"Then how do you know what it is?" He described the process they used to dye tumors to distinguish what kind they are.

"We're certain."

He began to tell me about survival rates. In teenagers, it can be as good as 70–80 percent with chemotherapy if there is only one tumor in one spot. For someone in middle age, the survival rate widened considerably: between 30–80 percent.

He recommended a standard fourteen-cycle course of chemo because Ewing's tends to seed microscopic, undetectable cancer cells into the blood. Chemo could push me closer to the 80 percent end of the survival spectrum. Treatment would require forty-nine days of chemo infusion altogether, with plenty of recovery time in between as the poison, developed for teenagers and their resilient bone marrow, would push my thirty-nine-year-old body to the brink: ten months altogether.

Dr. Butrynski listened patiently to all of our questions and answered them fully. Sometimes I sobbed. When I cried, he handed me tissues. He never looked at his watch, or cleared his throat, or answered his beeper, for two whole hours.

And when we finally fell silent, and a gigantic ball of congealing tissues replaced that sweet ball of hope in my lap, he asked gently, "Do you have any more questions?"

I did. "Are you a person of faith?"

"Yes."

Chapter 7

MANY ARE STRONG AT THE BROKEN PLACES

Ernest Hemingway once wrote that "the world breaks everyone and afterward many are strong at the broken places." He didn't write that *everyone* becomes strong at the broken places. Just that *many* are. What makes the difference between someone who is stronger at their broken places and someone whom the breaking just breaks?

I want to be careful here not to glamorize suffering or poverty. And I want to be careful not to conjure an image of a false God who sends tragedy upon us so that we can learn what we need to learn.

I don't believe that God is responsible for disasters and cancer, but that does not mean that our God is a safe God and won't ruthlessly take any opportunity to break and enter our hearts. We don't gather at my church on Sunday and shout, "God is Safe! All the time." We say: "God is Good/All the Time."

So many of us turn to God as a strong man, to keep us safe. But God is not safe, and love is not safe, and life is not safe. When Carmen was about seven, she found a baby bird in our vegetable bed one April. It was alive, but very frail. It had probably blown there out of a tree in the previous day's windstorm.

I was in the shower when I learned all this. Carmen came panting up three flights of stairs to alert me to the news. "Mom, it's amazing! I can see all its bones because it's naked! Can we try to help it?"

Naked? Visible skeletal structure? "Honey, I hate to tell you this, but it's probably going to die," I said as I soaped my feet unsteadily. "A lot of creatures and plants die in spring—they're just not strong enough to be here," I said.

Carmen looked skeptical and ran back downstairs. Between the shampoo and the rinse cycle, I heard her panting outside the shower again. "Mom, I've brought it to show you!" she said.

She'd gotten a plastic Tupperware and gently lifted the bird into it. It was, we were to learn, a nestling, eyes shut tight, all beak and bones and skinny butt, looking for all the world like an eighteen-week human ultrasound. It was alive. Shifting slightly, but not making a sound.

On that Easter in 2010, when I first knew the golf ball was there underneath my heart but before I could tell everybody, I preached about the egg, the life, the frailty of it all.

> *Spring is fragile; it's not safe and strong at the root like summer is. Spring blabs on and on about its "new life" this and "new life" that, but let's tell the truth: things that are trying to get born or give birth in spring, they don't always survive. Sometimes, the fruit trees bloom too early, and a killing frost arrives. The cow giving birth to her calf in the barn, the rabbit and her bunnies in the burrow, the woman in the maternity ward or the mud hut—they don't all make it. There are still whole cultures where children don't get their names until they are four or five years old, until they are summer-strong.*
>
> *There's a reason, after all, that we call it spring break. Of course, maybe that's the way God intended spring to be. Spring is Easter, and Easter means eggs. You wonder what Easter eggs have to do with the story of the Christian God coming to Earth as a human being, dying, and rising from the dead on the third day. It could be that the egg thing is just stolen outright from the Jews, who have an egg as a symbol of sacrifice on their Passover Seder plate, or from the pagans, who were deeply in tune with the rhythms of nature and our animal and springly desires to create and reproduce.*

But the story I was told as a child is that the egg is like the tomb Jesus was placed in—it looks like something quiet and dead, but really, there's a whole new life inside. We have to break the shell to get at it.

And often, something in us needs to break to get at new life.

Is it the breaking of things, then, that allows us to see God? That's how it happened for two disciples on the road to Emmaus, after Jesus died. They're walking along with Jesus for seven miles, talking to this man they knew like they knew their own faces, and didn't recognize him! It was only when something got broken—the bread, when they stopped to eat and rest for the night—that they recognized Jesus for who he was, and then he disappeared immediately.

This would sound like bad news, not good news, if it weren't for the fact that breaking of bread, in the Gospels, never happens by itself. Whenever Jesus fed people in our stories, the same four words appear, over and over. They are as close to magic words as we Christians get: Take. Bless. Break. Give. This is what Jesus did when fed the five thousand: he took the food, blessed it, broke it, gave it. He did it again when he fed the twelve disciples at the last supper. And he did it at the table in Emmaus. It's the same four words we say whenever we consecrate communion, our magic words.

God is not safe, but God is good. Nothing is broken that doesn't have a blessing behind it and a giving before it. What if it were true that everything that breaks in your life was bracketed by blessing and giving? What if believing it made it so, and we could stop being so afraid?

The news is so discouraging. There's so much hatefulness all around. When spit and racist epithets are hurled at icons of the civil rights movement because of a Senate vote on health care, there is something very broken in our country. When nine members of a Christian militia—how do those two words even go together in the *same phrase?—are arrested for plotting against the lives of innocent human beings in order to foment civil war, I see all these broken pieces. I'm overwhelmed by anger and want to throw them all away and start fresh.*

That's when God calls me back to this story, our story, the Easter story of the broken egg, the broken promises of friends, the broken body. God didn't throw away the pieces of this story, the failed Messiah, humiliated and dead on the cross, the runaway friends, the hypocritical priests.

God resurrected this body, complete with wounds, and showed how the breaking could offer a blessing. God did this two thousand years ago and God has been repeating the resurrection ever since. I've seen Her do it in your lives. When your hearts were broken or your cancer diagnosis came in or your dreams were desolated, I've seen you look behind the breaking for the blessing, and ahead of it to the giving. I've seen you notice God surrounding what's broken; I've seen you live to fall in love again, to go into remission, to get new and better dreams. How can I be so quick to throw away the broken bits I don't understand, when I have seen over and over, in the story of Jesus and in your stories, in this body of Christ, how much blessing and giving God does with the brokenness I do not understand?

Jesus practiced four verbs: take, bless, break, give. The angels gave humans one verb: Remember, is what they told the women in the garden. Remember what Jesus told you. Remember what he did, over and over. Take, bless, break, give.

Easter people, when something gets broken, look for Jesus immediately. Look behind the breaking to see what's being blessed, and look ahead to what God will give you.

I was afraid that chemo would break me and not bless me. I am not a particularly adventurous person. You will never catch me bungee-jumping or leaping out of a plane for the fun of it. As a teen, the most adventurous thing I did was get a perm that made me look like a fifty-year-old, and that was by accident.

So, confronted with the fact of chemo, I was deeply unnerved.

The idea of letting someone put a needle in my arm in order to pour in poisons designed to kill cells, including hair, stomach lining, mouth cells, white blood cells, red blood cells, and platelets, was anathema to me— tempting one death to avoid another. How could this thing that did such harm be any good? I wondered if the chemo was going to change me, fundamentally, at a cellular level.

And it would not only endanger me but also my family. One of the chemo drugs I was injected with, Adriamycin, also known as the Red Devil, came with a warning to put the lid down and flush the toilet twice after infusion. The toxins I was excreting could literally harm the people I shared a home with.

Before I started chemo, I had an idea about what the actual experience of the chemo infusion center would be like: half total boredom, half a cascade of glorious epiphanies showered upon you by salty nurses, devoted spouses, and especially the other cancer survivors, veterans lighting the way ahead for the newbies. Not to mention chicken salad sandwiches and ginger ale on demand, and no dishes to wash after.

I did meet radiant cancer patients on their second or third tour of duty, and alums in remission who just came back to hand out hugs to the staff. The chicken salad was great. And so were the nurses: kind and funny and brilliant and attentive. Chief among them, Kerry (you can't play favorites with nurses, but you can HAVE favorites).

Kerry had a mass of wavy black hair, thick black eyeliner, and a wisecracking patter that was hard to keep up with even when I wasn't compromised by IV drugs. She wore stilettos to work every day (just one more of her superpowers) and I still associate the clackety-clack of heels down a hospital hallway with the feeling that comfort and competence are on the way. She claimed me as her patient, and I claimed her as my port in the storm during the long hurricane that was treatment. She knew how to make me laugh, when to let me cry, and when to book me a private infusion room where she could shut the door and turn out the lights because the day was just too goddamn hard. I owe her a lion's share of my resurrection.

At first, chemo felt like a job I'd trained for my whole life. I'd bring my satchel filled with phytonutrient-rich treats, my eye mask, and my *Chemo, My Friend* guided meditation CD. At the end of every day, Kerry would take my IV out, I'd snip off the bracelet outing me as The Patient rather than The Helper or The Driver, and be free. Someone who could pass for normal. Get back to life. Maybe moving a little more slowly, a little queasy, but myself. The first day or two went like that. I seemed to recover by morning. I'd bounce into the infusion center, get vitals taken, pee in the cup, show off my great veins for a new IV, and get a bag of dextrose hung.

But by the fourth morning of a five-day-infusion week, I felt myself composed less of Molly and more of dark liquid, unable to swim to the surface.

F. Scott Fitzgerald said that in the dark night of the soul, it is always 3 a.m. I kept with me a folder full of loving emails from a parade of cheerleaders. But there are some 3 a.m.'s that the kindest and truest and most faithful of words can't reach when the dark liquid pulls you down to the bottom of the Mariana Trench.

Over the next 240 days, the dark liquid took me under, again and again. There were two thought-buoys I could latch myself to, to help me swim back to the surface. The first thought was that though my biochemically enchanted mind could not perceive it, the sunlit world was in fact as true and reliable as the dark liquid center in which I often found myself living.

The second thought was that I needed to find a median way through these storms, neither fighting to exhaustion nor giving up and drowning, but simply following the rhythm of the waves: observant, curious, as relaxed and trusting as possible. As each successive wave broke over me, I found myself amphibious: swimming deep and in the dark, and occasionally breaking the surface, shattering into sunlight.

We will all, again and again, suffer fragile springtimes. April showers can bring May shitstorms we don't believe we will withstand. But even shitstorms can be composted into "black gold." With enough time, and in the right conditions, the terrible things that happen to us can break down and become good soil rather than breaking us. Our tragedies need to be turned over and over, given oxygen and time, sifted free from sticks and stones, from the words and deeds and calamities that might have broken us, but, surprisingly, didn't.

Our foster son, Junior, has made me understand blessing after breaking like nobody else. When we first met him at coffee hour, he was a thirteen-year-old dead boy walking, weighing eighty pounds and so weak he could barely hold his head up because his heart was, quite literally, broken. He was newly arrived from Haiti to New England, where he would have lifesaving cardiac surgery to fix the ravages of rheumatic fever on his aortic valve.

Surgery turned him into a modern Tin Man with a titanium valve you could hear ticking away whenever the room grew quiet enough. His heart beat on even after his father, who had come as his guardian, abandoned him in the hospital to make a life for himself in the States. It beat on when child protective services determined he should not go back to Haiti because it might be a death sentence: his mother had previously sold his medication on the black market and he would now have to take coumadin for the rest of his life to avoid blood clots. So, he came to live with us in an emergency placement. It was winter, he was still convalescing, and now he was cold, homesick, and orphaned in a foreign country where he didn't speak the language.

Most days, while I worked from home so he wouldn't be alone with the ticking heart that I didn't yet quite trust to keep beating, he would watch *Kindergarten Cop* over and over. I felt powerless, with my bad high-school

French, to truly comfort or connect with him. I tried cooking for him, my love language, but he was an extremely picky eater and would only be satisfied by the hotdog omelets and Uncle Ben's Ready Rice he made for himself.

One night at dinner, we were eating in silence, not wanting to chatter away in English and leave Junior out of the conversation. Suddenly Carmen, age seven, let out an enormous toot. We all laughed uproariously, even Peter, who is normally fastidious about such things, and Junior along with us, until tears ran from our eyes. Carmen had found us a universal language.

As the weeks wore on, spring finally broke, and Boston Marathon Monday arrived. I took all three kids to Good Harbor Beach in Gloucester for the holiday to cavort in the sun when I got a text about bombers on the marathon route. They had blown up runners and cheerers in front of the historic church that had blessed those same runners in a worship service just the day before.

For days, the bombers eluded capture around the greater Boston area, and Friday night, as the chase escalated with a shelter-in-place order and a street-by-street manhunt not far from our home, Junior began vomiting. I threw him into the car and raced him through empty streets to Boston Children's Hospital.

Was it his heart? Had he thrown a clot? Was he having a stroke? When I got there, the obviously shaken ER staff told me that a bomb threat had been called into the hospital earlier by one of the Tsarnaev brothers. They didn't know if it was a false-flag operation, but they were proceeding with caution and would try to get Junior a CT scan as soon as possible.

As I sat in the waiting room, I prayed over and over, "Please, God, don't let Junior die on my watch." Had he survived everything only to expire in a terrorist attack on a children's hospital, or perhaps of a missed dose of coumadin because of his negligent foster mom?

But the CT scan came out fine. Junior was already feeling better. The doctor asked me about his diet, and suggested fewer hot dogs and more green vegetables.

He still hates green vegetables, but today, Junior is a tall, sharp, handsome, and hilarious young man with an infectious charm. When we moved, he found one, then another loving foster home, and a summer job as a lifeguard at the public pool, taking latchkey kids under his wing. He became both a baseball and a soccer star in high school and got recruited to a small college in Boston his senior year. He sometimes calls me Mom when he thinks I am not really listening, for which I am enormously grateful.

That doesn't mean his metaphorical heart is unbreakable. He is still able to be wounded: By the father he reconnected with in an uneasy truce after he surfaced a few years on with a new wife and baby. By the mother back in Haiti whom he sends remittances to from his job as a Zamboni driver, and who sometimes curses him for not sending more. Poverty and suffering can warp and distort us from the people we might otherwise be, and our parents are our first gods. When they act like assholes, it's easier to believe God is an asshole: an overbearing deity who is always disappointed or demanding from us what we can't give. Or: whimsical and unreliable, showing up and leaving again at inopportune moments.

Junior's quick laughter and zany antics belie a heart still a little broken at all that has happened to him, a heart defended against all the challenges that lie ahead for him, being young, Black, and an immigrant in America. But when I'm with him, and it's quiet, the titanium valve ticks reassuringly.

This year, we celebrated his twenty-first birthday by Zoom. From four rows of winking boxes, all the foster parents and bonus siblings who have loved him from that fragile springtime into his summer strength awkwardly sang to him and earnestly promised we would always be there for him. I pray he will remember he is not alone in the world and reach out for the help he needs, and the love he deserves, from the family he has made along the way.

We will not all emerge stronger at our broken places. The twinge, the ache, the limp, the hitch in our heart will forever remind us of what happened and that we are not the same on the other side of the thing that tried to end us, or took away someone we loved. Nor should we be. A heart that is broken is working exactly as it should. The real tragedy is a heart that has stopped feeling at all.

Chapter 8

THE SIN OF CERTAINTY

Close your eyes. See in your mind the homeless shelter for young adults ages sixteen to twenty-five nearest your home. Nearly half of the young people staying there, trying to rebuild their lives, are LGBTQ+. This doesn't even count the young adults not in shelter: those living on the streets or trading sex for a safer place to sleep. They are living rough for one primary reason: their fundamentalist parents banished them when they came out as queer. Their parents chose the cult of evangelical Christianity over their own children.

Banishment doesn't always result in homelessness. Exile can take many forms, including emotional and spiritual. In Somerville, our church was becoming known as a haven for young queer people who were deconstructing faith, but still loved God and the trappings of church. They craved its structure and support, as well as the chosen family they found there—and appreciated not just the acceptance but also the radical affirmation they found for who God had made them to be.

Isabella, Shanice, and Adam were still in an uneasy détente with their birth parents. Mom and Dad hadn't cut off their college tuition, and still welcomed them home for holiday meals, but the message was clear: I don't approve of you, and neither does God. Occasionally, some of those parents would wander cautiously into our sanctuary at their kids' invitation. They were surprised to see traditional pews, dark wood paneling, and a fairly conventional young straight mom wearing a black academic robe and stole rather than a bacchanalia of naked pagans worshipping goddesses (though that sounds fun).

At coffee hour, I sometimes took it upon myself to go over the antigay "clobber texts" of the Bible with those parents, trying to loosen up their sense of certainty in God and His judgments. I cited context for Deuteronomy, Leviticus, Romans, and I Corinthians, and noted that Jesus had hard words for those who judge and exclude others, but didn't have a thing to say about "the gays." I'm not sure my words did much good since earnest coffee-hour arguments don't usually break hard hearts or bend stiff necks. What does that is relationship, over time: a parent deciding to let their natural love rather than ideology win. But I hoped that words from an ally, and one with some religious authority, would be a little shovel into stony soil, breaking it up and preparing it for a new idea to sprout.

Then again, those parents weren't wrong: occasionally, our sanctuary *was* transformed into a wild bacchanalia of joy. Like at our annual Drag Gospel Festival, a fundraiser for gay and trans refugees from countries like Uganda and Jamaica, where to be queer is a death sentence.

Serenity Jones, our drag-queen-in-residence, invited her professional drag friends every year to perform in the overflowing sanctuary to raucous applause, laughter, and tears. Queer and straight, we all delighted in an opportunity to gender-bend, whether we were performing or pew-sitting: straight men in church-lady hats and smoky eyes, soccer moms with fake mustaches—even the babies were in drag. Our abundant harvest of church children hooted and leaped with joy. We stepped out of the stream of ordinary time and into kairos, Kin-dom time.

A few minutes into worship one year, I noticed our associate pastor Jeff, a bearded, brawny, and tenderhearted former community organizer who could both weep publicly without shame and face down wealthy, bullying Manhattan restaurateurs with steely resolve, sitting uncharacteristically rigid in his chair, staring out, even as bits of feather boas were flying through the air around him. What could possibly be the matter?

I leaned over to him. "What's wrong with you?" I asked.

He unobtrusively pointed. "That guy over there," he answered. "Front pew. Left side. He's very angry, and agitated."

"I'll put the deacons on notice," I said.

"No, it's probably okay."

"I'll do it anyhow," and I moved easily, smiling, toward the back, in my Pope costume.

Liz had seated herself next to the angry interloper with willful, joyful, five-year-old Nora, who had narrowly dodged being flattened by a giant tree the previous year. Nora, who had zero shyness with strangers, now climbed over him, trying to get to the exit, shattering his self-imposed isolation.

I found Deacon Jeffrey and Deacon Marlin in the back, pointed him out, and asked them to move closer and observe. We saw his lips moving. Was he rehearsing a speech? Was he so spitting mad his brain couldn't contain the words? Was he hearing voices from somewhere else telling him to act?

I asked Peter to move in too, feeling physical pain that I was asking my husband, my heart, to potentially put himself in harm's way. As Jeff started reading scripture, I sat next to our twenty-seven-year-old moderator, Ian. I took his hand and asked him to pray with me. "That man—he's angry. I'm not sure what he's going to do," I said.

Because the week before: three mass shootings at college campuses.

And the previous summer: Dylann Roof killed nine people in their own church for being Black.

And previous to that: that shooting in the Unitarian church, people killed for being liberal Christians.

I held Ian's hand, and I prayed to God for protection. "I know you didn't protect those people in Charleston, South Carolina, Lord, the people who loved their enemy and talked to him for an hour, humanizing themselves. I know you loved them as much as you love us, and you couldn't or wouldn't protect them, but I'm asking you: please be our shield against hatred and those who would hurt us."

I prayed, and Rev. Jeff read this scripture aloud, which I have never heard before in its splendor:

If God is for us, who is against us? The One who did not withhold Her own Son, but gave Him up for all of us, will She not with Him also give us everything else? Who will bring any charge against God's elect? It is God who justifies. Who is to condemn? It is Christ Jesus, who died, yes, who was raised, who is at the right hand of God, who indeed intercedes for us. Who will separate us from the love of Christ? Will hardship, or distress, or persecution, or famine, or nakedness, or peril, or sword?…

No, in all these things we are more than conquerors through The One who loved us. For I am convinced that neither death, nor life, nor angels, nor rulers, nor things present, nor things to come, nor powers, nor height, nor depth, nor anything else in all creation will be able to separate us from the love of God in Christ Jesus our Lord.

I felt the air heavy with spiritual power. Magic was present.

That was when the man stood up, slowly, as if summoned by the scripture. He stepped over the front pew into the free space. Turning toward us, he began shouting.

"You have painted Christ like a prostitute!"

As if in a pre-rehearsed dance, Marlin and Jeffrey and Peter and Dan and Keith and Steve moved in on him, closing the circle. They touched him gently, patting him down, containing him the way you would a toddler who is acting out, keeping him from hurting himself or others while not getting hurt oneself.

At least that was the hope. Because when they stood up and stepped in, there was no way of knowing if he was armed. These men—these gentle, wonderful men—some of them the fathers of young children—interposed their bodies, willingly, to protect us.

And Rev. Jeff, his face painted to look exactly like the genderqueer twelfth-century Jesus icon of our photoshopped drag gospel poster, walked down from the chancel and stood about fifteen feet away from him. Ablaze with the spirit of a Hebrew prophet, Jeff said loudly to our men, "I want your hands off of him. Get your hands off of him."

The man had a name tag on. Perhaps some part of him wanted to be known. Jeff called him by name. "Drew, Drew, I want you to know that I love Jesus too. I love and honor the person of Jesus, down in my soul."

I went over to support Jeff, and standing about ten feet behind him, I held up my hands—in blessing, in support, the way you would put your hands up behind someone you're afraid is going to fall.

I couldn't let Jeff stand there alone and was worried that Drew might intend us physical harm. Later, I went over the scene in my mind a thousand times: how grateful I was that I wasn't the one who was on the chancel when Drew started his speech. How grateful I wasn't the one who had to find the words, and present my armorless body.

Jeff continued. "I want you to look at these people," he directed Drew. "This is the face of some of God's children."

Jeff looked. Drew looked. I looked out over the congregation. No one was fleeing (even though they had good reason to). The atmosphere was now tense and terrifying. The flying feathers were all on the ground, and the children, instead of running around and climbing over pews, were still. Everyone was sitting, alert. Then hands began to go up, in blessing—first a few, then dozens, open palms sending peace toward Drew.

They have been practicing blessing for so long. Every previous act of blessing: backpacks and babies, offering envelopes and Peace Corps volunteers, low-wage workers getting robbed by their companies and LGBT asylum seekers—had been leading up to this moment, this Blessing 2.0, this ninja-level blessing of the enemy while he is in the act of cursing you.

Jeff and Drew continued to talk at a distance, Drew spooling out his speech, Jeff answering him in love but with healthy boundaries. Finally, Jeff said, "You've said what you've come to say. You've been heard. Now it's time for you to go."

"But one other thing," Jeff said. "Look at me."

Drew looked into that turquoise-shadowed, red-lipsticked, genderqueer Jesus face, a mirror of the poster that had brought him to our door that day. And here's what Drew had to listen to that Jesus say directly to him.

"I love you."

Then Drew, turning to face us, said, "I love you too; I love all of you."

Afterward, someone told me they heard him add, "Please forgive me." But I'm not sure that's true.

With that, Drew left. Keith and Marlin and Peter accompanied him down the side stairs, where he started sobbing. He walked away toward Davis Square. Deacon Erica had called the cops, and they arrived a few minutes later.

When he was out of sight, the congregation clapped and cheered, but Jeff stayed the cheering with a raised hand. This was a moment of relief, but not a moment of triumph over another human being. We would not shame him as he left, weeping.

And then our guest preacher, Rev. Day, a queer Black lesbian UCCer with Pentecostal sensibilities, got up and preached her heart out. It was all about Love. About not just ordinary human love but God's kind of "gonna STAY with us no matter WHAT" love. And she broke into song, "Ain't no mountain high enough," and we sang back, "Ain't no valley low enough." And we all sang, "Ain't no river wide enough … keep me from getting to you, Babe." She preached like nobody's business and we waved our hands in the air, and hollered back, and hollered out our fear and our adrenaline, our courage and our joy.

When it was time to take the offering for queer asylum seekers, King Jean Pierre from Cameroon gave his testimony. He told us how he had been cut and burned, robbed and hounded away from his village, away from his role as a tribal leader, away from family, home, and all his worldly possessions. He told us about almost losing his life. We caught a momentary taste of what it is to suffer for your beliefs and your identity and the identity of those you love and stand (and pray, sing, dance) with.

And we gave. We gave $7,500 that day, our scrappy little church, for the lives of queer refugees.

The closing song was a meditation called "Breathe In, Breathe Out," and that's exactly what it helped us do. We sang it over and over and let the stress hormones leave our bodies.

And then we had a dance party. Because sometimes that's just what God's people need.

———

Some people never outgrow fundamentalist thinking. Morally, they remain children, stuck in "good guys and bad guys" binary thinking, but they have adult power, access to media and privilege and weapons, making them as dangerous as a toddler with a gun.

Some understand themselves to be Jesus's agents on Earth, and some believe that the violence they commit is authorized at the highest levels because they are in a holy war. When Christian fundamentalism morphs into Christian nationalism, it supports an agenda that has nothing to do with Jesus and everything to do with white supremacy, control over women's bodies, rigid gender constructs, and violence against the earth itself.

Fundamentalism, with its self-reinforcing, self-righteous certainties, is a sin because it claims to know the mind of God, and who can know that?

All claims to the contrary, Jesus did not preach from a place of rigid binaries and judgments but from a place of continual becoming. He befriended outcasts and lived on the margins of society while staying in relationship with wealthy and powerful people, some of whom became patrons and disciples. He lived in a patriarchal society, but let women correct him and expand his understanding of his mission. Innocent of the trumped-up charges, he allowed himself to be murdered by state violence to expose the injustice of that violence. He asked us to love our enemies, and to bless those who curse us. He warned that those who lived by the sword would die by it.

The churches I've served strive to follow Jesus in this "third way": neither returning evil for evil nor caving in to it. Our God does not hate all the same people we do, nor does our God particularly want us to be rich or admired. Our faith, frail as it is sometimes, is also flexible. It is self-correcting as we have profound encounters with people who are different from us and are exposed to new experiences and ideas. If we are willing to be humble, we can continuously root out our own biases, the weeds of white supremacy that are deeply seeded into the soil of our culture, religion, and country.

Staying in the liminal place of holy uncertainty is deeply uncomfortable. But certainty in the life of faith doesn't serve us well. At some point, the idea or theology or God-image we have adopted may become provably false. Then we'll have to decide to double down on it or abandon it, which may feel like abandoning God or faith altogether, and leave us entirely unmoored.

People worry so much about doubting. Frederick Buechner said, "Doubts are the ants in the pants of faith. They keep it alive and moving."

I recently asked Ashley, who first decided God was an asshole as a teen, how her faith was evolving. She has gone through a long season of wrestling with what faith is, exactly, if it's not allegiance to the veracity of ancient texts—recognizing that they have been cherry-picked and translated by people (ahem, men) with subjective worldviews and political agendas. She was helped by another minister along the way who told her that science is the study of the known and religion is the study of the unknown. Throughout time, what is unknown and known shifts.

She said, "There is so much unknown to us as humans, and I can just have faith that God is not an asshole, which has alleviated decades-long anxieties. This is still an uncomfortable place for me to be in, but I've become comfortable with the discomfort and the unknown."

Getting cancer can make a fundamentalist out of even an atheist, although the adopted religion is probably more likely to be raw foodism or colloidal silver than Christianity. In the Early Cancer Era, I read all the cheerful "heal yourself with wheatgrass shots and positive thinking" books, hoping to take some agency back. Getting a difficult diagnosis messes with your thinking in all kinds of good ways, but also bad, or at least not useful, ways. It sends your mind onto flights of fancy, looking for reasons and answers. It's where fundamentalism can form, looking for easy answers, definite villains, a ten-step path to nirvana.

Why did I get cancer? I wondered in the early days. Did I give myself cancer by stress and worry? By not releasing a past trauma? Eating too many Lindt truffles? Was it my two-pack-a-day mother's fault? Or a forgiveness I've withheld that has toxified and corroded my tissues?

Plenty of literature out there aids and abets stinkin' thinking about cancer. But it is not really helpful for a new cancer patient to hear that you can spontaneously heal yourself if you just let go of negative emotions (Uh, Ch'YAH, you just got a cancer diagnosis! You're going to have negative emotions!).

Not to denigrate the really fine work of many healers. But this advice does often, especially to the newly diagnosed person, come off as making us feel responsible for giving ourselves cancer, which is patently bullshit. Let's all just admit that.

Cancer just HAPPENS. It happens to "good people" and to "bad people," to fat and thin, to angry and happy, to healthy eaters and junk-food-junkies, to people of faith and agnostics and atheists.

I also asked the question: "Why not *them?*" "Why not that person who eats hotdogs for breakfast? Or that person who is so clearly filled with vit-riol and bad will that it seeps out of every pore when they are in traffic?" It was curiosity more than judgment—shouldn't these things poison them and make them way more likely than me to get cancer? It echoes Jeremiah's cry to God, "Why do the wicked prosper?"

We are all amateur fundamentalists because we all want reasons. Reasons mean rules, and rules mean we can avoid bad things happening to ourselves and those we love. The wanting of reasons can lead us into magical think-ing—*I thought X, therefore X happened. I am so powerful!* It is the hallmark of small children—preschool age, but occasionally older children, and of course, altogether too many adults.

A few weeks into my diagnosis, I read a chapter from *Raising an Emotion-ally Healthy Child When a Parent Is Sick* that encouraged me to "remind your child, who is prone to magical thinking, that he or she did not cause your illness by thinking bad thoughts or being angry with you."

I realized that as much as we had talked about it, I hadn't told Rafe and Carmen those exact words. I'd sort of assumed Carmen was too young and upbeat and Rafe, too mature and rational, to believe that they'd caused my cancer. Then I remembered that just a few weeks before the diagnosis came in, miffed at some outrageous meanness of mine like making him brush his teeth before bed, Rafe had said, "I am going to pray to God that you die in the night!"

So, on the walk to school the day after I read that chapter, I casually mentioned to him, "Just so you know, it is nobody's fault that I have cancer. Nothing you said, or did, or failed to do, gave me cancer."

He stopped in his tracks, looked at me with surprise, and said, "Why didn't you tell me this earlier?"

Oh, dear Jesus.

Now I had a second conundrum to deal with. Rafe is smart and would soon have figured out on his own that (1) if his negative thoughts can't give me cancer then (2) maybe his positive thoughts, i.e., prayers, can't make me cancer-free.

So, I followed up, "Here is the thing, honey. Because God is all goodness, peace, joy, wholeness—God *can't* respond to the negative thoughts—it is not in God's nature to make me die in the night just because you asked for it.

"But because God is good, our prayers for healing or anything good tap into the energy that is trying to put all the good things back together that got broken." I hope that I was adequately explaining prayer as *tikkun olam*—the Jewish concept of healing, repair, and transformation of the world.

When I moved on to Carmen for the magical thinking conversation, she just nodded briskly and went back to singing and scribbling, as if to say: "I know, Mom. How could anybody as cheerful and helpful as I am *possibly* give anybody cancer?"

Both of my kids are intensely spiritual in different ways. Carmen has more certainty and fewer doubts, but that's her nature in all things. For example, the interjection "Oh, my God" is verboten in our house. I don't care—much—if the kids drop the f-bomb, but we don't like them to talk about God in an offhand way.

When Carmen accidentally said it as a little one, she would pause, ask God's forgiveness, put one ear to the sky, and after a respectful moment, say, "She said 'I forgive you,'" then go on with whatever she was doing.

Rafe, on the other hand, has always been plagued with doubts about lots of things in general, and God in particular. When he was five years old and we were crossing the street in Davis Square, he said philosophically, "I'm not sure if I believe Jesus is God. I mean, how can God pray to God?" Fourteen years later, he still hasn't worked out his Trinitarian theology.

But his doubt means he takes it all so much more seriously. "It all" being in this case the notion of a good God, and along with that notion, the possibility—no, the reality—of evil. If the divinity of Jesus is in question, evil is most certainly not, in Rafe's mind. When he was little, we had many a bad night sitting vigil against the powers of darkness.

Carmen, on the other hand, was an Evil Denier, at least until she got her first cell phone and started reading the news. For a whole year, Carmen forbade us from saying the entire Lord's Prayer. Whenever we arrived at "Deliver us from evil," we had to omit "from evil." To say it would give it power and reality. After all, God spoke Creation into being—"Let there be light!" and there was light. Words engender reality.

I myself have always been a bit of a Pollyanna when it comes to evil. Sure, I believe in it. I'm an orthodox Christian, and that's what we do. But I return to C.S. Lewis on evil, for his sensible ideas about it without being fundamentalist and reductionist.

> *One of the things that surprised me when I first read the New Testament seriously was that it talked so much about a Dark Power in the universe—a mighty evil spirit who was held to be the Power*

behind death and disease, and sin. The difference is that Christianity thinks the Dark Power was created by God, and was good when it was created, and went wrong. Christianity agrees with Dualism that this universe is at war. But it does not think this is a war between independent powers. It thinks this is a civil war, a rebellion, and that we are living in a part of the universe occupied by the rebel.

Enemy-occupied territory—that is what this world is. Christianity is the story of how the rightful king has landed, you might say landed in disguise, and is calling us all to take part in a great campaign of sabotage. When you go to church you are really listening in to the secret wireless from our friends: that is why the enemy is so anxious to prevent us from going. He does it by playing on our conceit and laziness and intellectual snobbery.

Enemy-occupied territory. Eventually, I talked Carmen into understanding that by *not* speaking of Evil—The E That Must Not Be Named—we were actually giving it more power and putting ourselves in its thrall. Together, we evolved into saying evil loudly and powerfully, like secret agents communicating a message on the wireless, to God, and all of those on the side of Light.

⁀

I recently taught a Confirmation class on one of my favorite topics: heaven, hell, sin, and grace. Carmen, now fifteen, happens to be in the class. The good news is, the confirmands said they mostly don't believe in hell. The bad news is, they also don't believe in heaven. I couldn't even sway them with my super-compelling case for Universalism robbed from the end of C.S. Lewis's *The Last Battle.*

Because these young people are on their own spiritual journeys, their own paths to becoming, they don't need to believe what I believe. For some of the confirmands who have developed a finely tuned sense of cynicism and self-preservation, I do lament the lack of magic, mystery, wonder, and openness to a different reality than what they perceive. Although it's certainly understandable they might choose cynicism as a defense mechanism given that they have been raised on a steady diet of school shootings, climate chaos, and Trumpism.

But even atheism and agnosticism can be a form of fundamentalism—a refusal to be taken in, even by that which wants to offer you everything, without asking for a thing in return.

Chapter 9

LIFE IS LOVE SCHOOL

Every heart, every heart
To love will come
But like a refugee
　　　　—Leonard Cohen, "Anthem"

Author and mystic Fr. Richard Rohr calls life "Love School." We're put here not to work and prove our value to the earthly enterprise, as I sometimes imagine, nor to build masterpieces that will outlive us, as I also sometimes imagine, nor to sit on the couch and watch bad TV and eat cheese puffs, as I *also* sometimes imagine. The main reason we are here, I've decided after five decades of fieldwork, is to learn how to love.

Some of us are not very good at it. We didn't get a great start in life. We didn't have good teachers, and how do you become an auto-didact at love? Or we're born with differently wired brains and need to practice empathy as well as learn how to read (and even experience) emotion.

I don't know which one Carl was: traumatized or somewhere on the spectrum, or neither, or both. I only know that when he died, he was an enormously different person than the one I met when I first arrived at First Church Somerville.

He was a thin white man in his sixties with strange, faraway, blue eyes that made me feel odd whenever they landed on me. Though he lived alone and didn't drive, he wouldn't allow himself to ride to church with married women unless their husbands were present. He went to sleep every day at three in the afternoon. He frequently seemed to be in some sort of dream state at meetings, rarely saying a word. His face seemed like it was permanently fixed on the Dour setting.

The only thing worse than his grim silence was when he actually opened his mouth. I've mentioned our church practice of inviting people to give a spiritual testimony during worship. With our brilliant and emotionally intelligent cast of characters, their stories often made us laugh, cry, and grow by leaps and bounds.

But then came the Sunday when Carl stood on the chancel and talked at length about murderous homosexual chimpanzees to a polite, stunned crowd who had no idea what he was talking about. Was he homophobic? Or just watching too much late-night cable TV? When he was finished, he obviously thought he had killed it because, with more enthusiasm than I'd ever seen in him, he asked me if next time he could preach a whole sermon.

One time, I visited his apartment to bring him an Easter lily. I won't lie. Even though he'd never given me actual cause to fear him, he triggered some primal survival instinct. I told Peter where I was going and when. If I was going to be cut into tiny pieces and disappeared into the Mystic River, I wanted someone to know who the chief suspect was.

The lily and I entered an apartment as strange as he was. It most closely resembled a cut-rate dentist's office. A perfectly sterile galley kitchen. Empty bookshelves dividing the main room in two. A tidy stack of outdated magazines. No art, no photos, nothing to give any indication of who this person was, what or whom he cared about. After we made some stilted conversation, I left, feeling sad (and more curious than ever).

What did he get out of church? He was regular in his habits, never late to a deacons' meeting, diligent in the execution of his duties. I wondered why someone who was such a creature of habit, and so rigidly religious, hung out at a church that was growing younger, more madcap and colorful, and ever queerer—though not his kind of queer.

About two years after first meeting him, I noticed something happening. He was becoming softer and more open. He smiled more (which took some getting used to). He started cracking jokes with three-year-old Rafe. He let me touch his arm, warmly, even if Peter wasn't present.

He volunteered to become a welcomer, which at first made my heart quail—every new member at our little church was hard-won, and this felt like inviting a gargoyle to guard the gate. But Carl took this role as seriously as the others: he welcomed the instruction to learn people's names, use their names in conversation so they felt known, and accompany them to coffee hour if they were too shy to go on their own.

One day, a new woman came to church, and she looked so comfortable with Carl, I thought they might be old friends. I asked her about it. "No," she said, "I just met him this morning, and he was very welcoming."

When our baby boom came a few years later, fourteen babies born in five months, he was in heaven. He befriended Liz, the one who had struggled so hard to feel the presence of God in her miscarriage. Soon, she was the one bringing him a lily every Easter, with her two rambunctious children in tow, and they developed an unlikely friendship.

There is no earthly reason, no convincing theory (as much as I believe in neuroscience as one of God's Morse codes to us), why someone whose personality and habits were as set as Carl's should change. And yet with each year, he did. When he later died, many in the congregation turned out for his funeral. Their grief for him was genuine, as was their gratitude for what he so intentionally gave to the church.

It's the Carls of the world, as much as any personal mystical experience, that have reinforced my faith that God is real. If Carl can go to Love School so late in life, there's hope for you and me.

Another Love School pupil was Julie, from my church in Berkeley. She's lived nine lives, and has at least a few more left. She grew up in the South with Kentucky Derby bonnets and mint juleps, ran off to be a rock singer in LA in her twenties, then went to law school and became an ass-kicking litigator. She met and married a dashing Filipino architect, Lorenzo, in a DIY wedding in our humble parish hall. They had two sweet babies. Their marriage didn't last, but they worked out joint custody of both their kids and the church, and to this day, they share the front pew.

At one point, Julie shared part of her story about our church and her faith.

> *Divorce is never easy, and it certainly wasn't for us—it was hard on our children and hard on us as parents and spouses. Over the months, we struggled. This church family listened without judgment as we mourned and raged, let us weep, counseled us, and finally dried our tears. Little by little, with the help of our church family and a great deal of the Holy Spirit, we were able to form a new and different kind of "nuclear" family, forged of forgiveness and compassion.*
>
> *In 2016, I suffered a near-fatal car accident while traveling in Southern California. While I was stuck six hours from home undergoing surgeries over many weeks, Lorenzo and the church stepped up and made sure the kids were fully fed, cared for, reassured, and comforted. I came home to find that Lorenzo and our church family had been hard at work rearranging my entire house to make sure it was wheelchair accessible, and in the following weeks, so many delicious meals were delivered to me that my freezer was overflowing. Lorenzo and our church family have never stopped stepping up when needed, as continuing surgeries have sidelined me a number of times in the years since.*
>
> *While Lorenzo and I are no longer romantic partners and no longer share one household, we are now bound by deeper and more spiritual ties: love of God, our children, our church family, and even one another, just in a different way.*

Just a few months before the accident, God tumbled a new love into Julie and Lorenzo's life. A former lover of Lorenzo's showed up on his doorstep with the one-year-old son he had not known about, conceived after his split from Julie. The baby's mother was in a severe mental health crisis, serially homeless, and unable to care for Abie, and she left him with Lorenzo, never to return.

Abie started tagging along to Julie's when it was her night with their kids, Talyn and Josie, and within a few months, he was calling her Mom. It helped that Abie was a winsome, exuberant child, delighted by everything. But even given how helpless she was against his charms, I am stunned at the moxie it took for Julie to say yes to this unexpected love in her life. To say yes to becoming a mother again in the most unexpected way, as a single parent, an ex, and finally, a person who was newly disabled.

I could believe Julie's press and chalk it up to the fact that she and her family had a great church. But the fact is, she made a choice to make her heart bigger, and her life more complicated, in staying friends with Lorenzo and falling in love with Abie.

All of us are tribal by nature. It's an evolutionary survival mechanism. But Jesus calls us to expand our sense of tribe until everybody's in. That's the work of Love School. Richard Rohr in *The Universal Christ* wrote, "A mature Christian sees Christ in everything and everyone else. That is a definition that will never fail you, always demand more of you, and give you no reasons to fight, exclude, or reject anyone."

One time a clergy friend, Laura Ruth, said with heavy exasperation, "There are people I want to hate, but then they tell me their stories, and then I know them, and then I can't help but love them." There are now whole YouTube channels, StoryCorps sites, and Facebook groups for learning the stories of out-group people we want to judge or hate. There are also purple churches—or even royal blue churches like mine, where pink-haired trans activists share the pews with retired UC Berkeley professors—helping us earn our doctorate in Love School.

(Then again, sometimes it's the people you are closest to who are hardest to love. As my bestie Aisha says, be kindest to the people who can kill you in your sleep and leave no evidence.)

Ordination in my tradition requires candidates to write a comprehensive paper outlining a holistic take of their religious beliefs. Not all of my own big theological concepts have held up since I wrote mine twenty-five years ago, but this one has: my core belief that God is real. I quoted Saint Mahalia Jackson (singing Kenneth Morris's gospel song) in my paper:

> *There are some things*
> *I may not know*
> *There are some places*
> *I can't go*
> *But I'm sure*
> *Of this one thing*
> *That God is real*
> *For I can feel*
> *Him deep within.*

I also quoted the Skin Horse, via author Margery Williams's *The Velveteen Rabbit*. He teaches the rabbit that we are not born real. It is the love of others that makes us real—and the process can hurt.

> *"Does it happen all at once, like being wound up," the Rabbit asked, "or bit by bit?"*
> *"It doesn't happen all at once," said the Skin Horse. "You become. It takes a long time. That's why it doesn't happen often to people who break easily, or have sharp edges, or who have to be carefully kept. Generally, by the time you are Real, most of your hair has been loved off, and your eyes drop out and you get loose in the joints and very shabby. But these things don't matter at all, because once you are Real you can't be ugly, except to people who don't understand."*

It isn't we who make God more real by loving Her. It is God who makes us more real by putting people in our path who we can choose to love and be loved by. The realer we grow, the more profoundly and blessedly can we comprehend the Really Real that is God.

Frankly, being loved is almost as hard as loving because it requires a degree of trust and surrender that is absolutely terrifying to our carefully constructed egos. And it's the work of Love School.

⌒

It's a cliché to say that becoming a parent is the best shot most of us have at unlocking new and ninja love-levels in Love School. What they don't tell you is that it will also take you to new levels of fury, disappointment, anxiety, and stone-cold terror.

Carmen has always been my easy kid. She is the entertainer, the cuddler, the creature of supernatural levels of empathy who can't see a Lost Dog sign stapled to a telephone pole or we will all drown in the vale of tears that follows.

Rafe is my study in paradoxes. He is affectionate and cynical, intellectual and a goofball. He has few friends his own age, but counts among his closest pals his paternal grandmother, an eighty-year-old spiritual director from our church who calls him regularly because she loves to talk philosophy with him, and the homeless alcoholic who sleeps outside of the restaurant where he works.

Despite being the firstborn, he is not a rule-follower, but a risk-taker. Even as a little one, he shouldered the role of Wayward Preacher's Kid, experimenting with matches in the sanctuary after church, or crawling the length of the pews buck naked in the middle of worship, or absconding with the best goodies from the coffee hour table to play "Food Spies" with the other children in his thrall on the back stairs.

As he grew, the risks he took became progressively riskier, from riding his bike in the dark without a helmet or lights to experimenting with substances and getting into fights. The kindergartner who insisted I buy him a sparkle heart shirt from the girls' section at Target was bullied for wearing his heart so openly. So he slammed it shut. The bullying, unbeknownst to me and Peter at the time, continued for years. He grew into a boy who would sleep with a steak knife tucked into his mattress because it made him feel safer. A part of him continued to feel uneasy in the world, and that's why he came at it so hard—it's safer to be on the offensive than the defensive.

As parents, a mistake we made for a long time with Rafe was trying to control him and deny his dissident impulses rather than let him be a whole person with all kinds of feelings and fears, who learns from his own mistakes rather than from our stern warnings.

We outlawed the *avada kedavra* curse during his Harry Potter phase. We forbade guns and he turned every stick into a pretend firearm. Trying too hard to fit him into the box of who we wanted him to be, we missed out on so much of who he, in fact, already was. When his grades plummeted from As to Fs in middle school, we thought he was lazy. It wasn't until he begged for testing three years later that we found out he had ADD.

But years before the ADD diagnosis, when I was in the short, curly, chemo hair phase of recovery, I wrote this in my journal:

> I was downright mean to Rafe last night, on the eve of his birthday. The boy took seventy-five minutes to do his homework. Three minutes of that was actual-homework time. The other seventy-two minutes were for making fart noises, singing in an annoying falsetto, falling out of his chair, and grousing about how much he hates homework.
>
> I was exhausted, and I said mean things to him. Mean, manipulative things about the importance of Taking Care of His Responsibilities Like Homework and therefore helping me keep my stress low so my cancer wouldn't come back. His eyes actually filled with tears when I said this.
>
> I told you. MEAN. I'm so ashamed. And, apparently, I'm just like everybody else who goes through this cancer shit, it turns out—scared when treatment ends, and it is just you and your body and its invisible cell-churning mysteries again, the future unknowable and stretched out before you, and God just as inscrutable and making no promises.

The summer before, in the middle of a getaway from chemo to Les and Sam's flower farm, I was in the hammock when God came and had words with me about Rafe.

I had been praying about Rafe because he'd said so often that Peter and I were mean, and he didn't think Peter loved him, and implied I didn't like him very much either. I attributed some of it to his age and some to his anxiety around my diagnosis. I assumed that it would pass with time.

But then an intrusive thought clanged my heart. What if this is not eight-year-old-developmental-stuff, or cancer, but this is really our kid, and we're pushing each other away, moving inexorably apart? What if his feeling that Peter or I don't like him doesn't pass but deepens, corrodes? And I don't realize till it's too late?

I thought about what to do. I'd already tried telling him that no matter how he *feels*, the reality is that we love him very much, and love means setting limits, especially parents for children. But who in the history of mortals has ever given up their feelings because they've seen the rational merit of the other person's position?

I thought about the year I was eight. I was living at my father's house and miserable because of how unfairly I felt my stepmother treated me compared to my half brother Jesse, her bio child. My dad didn't seem to notice, let alone protect or defend me. It was very painful to feel less loved. It was a Cinderella moment, and I carried those wounds with me for a long time, until my stepmother and I later became friends in adulthood.

God said, "Maybe you should consider that Rafe is right. Not that you don't love him—of course you love him. But that you don't always like him. That you're not quite sure what to do with him. That you take care of the needs of his body, but you don't have a real, healthy interest in his mind, imagination, his boy-ness that you are so mystified by, and maybe a little frightened by. Yeah, yeah, you sometimes pretend to be interested in his prattle about Poptropica or Minecraft, but he's smart enough to know that you're faking it. He thinks you're gentler on Carmen, that she never gets 'in trouble,' that she is easier. He sees you take her onto your lap a thousand times a day, joke about winning the gold in the Cuddling Olympics. And he believes that translates into you loving her more.

"Rafe doesn't need the same things from you that Carmen does. But he does need to know, unequivocally, how much you love him and approve of him, even before he has earned it. Because he can't earn it. And he shouldn't have to."

God didn't say all that, but, let's say, heavily *implied* it as the sun set over the valley.

I listened. And I cried, because it was true. I resolved to try. To cuddle more, and not just nominally. To listen, carefully, and perhaps find myself being interested.

Les and Sam, and so many adults in our lives, are good at listening to Rafe, and it brings out the best in him. The day before my hammock musings, Sam and Rafe had lunch together, and I had eavesdropped on their conversation about Afghanistan and multiple wives, and when we left to go back to Somerville, Sam said, "Rafe, talking with you at lunch yesterday was the highlight of my day," and Rafe earnestly said, "Me too." I realized how much I wanted back the closeness we had when he was very small. Not only that, I wanted it *forward*.

The next day, I made a new beginning. God can do so much with just a little effort. We went to a local pond, and he ran around it, and I swam the length of it, and we met on the other side and explored there. I invited him onto the hammock with me to watch the spider hunt flies. I got one kid who was tough, and one who was tender. I love them both so much it hurts. One brought out my own toughness, the other my tenderness. I didn't realize how much they both needed that tenderness.

That divine talking-to was the beginning of a change for me, but not the beginning of long-term ease for us as a family. Rafe continued to be one of my chief challengers and also best spiritual teachers. ADD meds didn't solve all our problems, though they helped. So did discovering he needed glasses and had sleep apnea, two more ways he advocated for himself when we assumed he was just not trying hard enough. But, along with the self-advocacy, there was also self-sabotage that brought him and us to some pretty low places.

During my first hospitalization with neutropenia, in July of chemo year, we wouldn't let Carmen come visit. We thought it would be too scary for her, seeing me so frail in a place of sickness and dying. But Rafe came. He crawled right into the narrow bed next to me, bald, gray in pallor, sprouting plastic tubing from various body parts, and hung on tight. Together, we watched *Monsters, Inc*, giggling at the antics and sighing together at the end, and the moral of the story: tenderness and laughter create much more power than fear.

We're still in Love School, all four of us. And we will never graduate.

Chapter 10

GOD DOESN'T HAVE A PLAN, BUT GOD HAS A DREAM

Between stimulus and response, there is a space. And in that space lies our power to choose. And in our choice lies our growth and our freedom.
—attributed to Victor Frankl

I was walking down the street on a sunny May afternoon a few weeks after Dr. B. told me the way the next year of my life was going to go when I got a call from my sister Tessa. Tessa is younger than me by nine years, and a free spirit. She was my first child in many ways: when she was two and I was eleven, I would pack her into her umbrella stroller and take her on long walks to the park, library, and Baskin-Robbins so our mom could have a break.

When she would wander out of the house by herself, it would be me who searched the neighborhood for her high and low, sometimes finding her making mud pies in the playground across the street, other times blocks away. Tessa was always entirely her own person: a fairy, a dreamer, an artist, an enfant terrible, both personally powerful and dreadfully defenseless.

On this sunny afternoon, Tessa called me from the tent on Kauai where she was living with her partner, a raw milk farmer. She can be frustratingly wackadoodle with her potions and conspiracy theories, but on this day, Tessa was at her wisest and most loving. Not being fundamentalist about raw food strategies or dark energy, just gently offering suggestions.

"Essiac tea," she said to me. "Maybe try some maitake mushrooms and raw milk." Also, she said quietly, she would be thrilled to send me some local organic weed and ginger. "Spirit told me that you should be smoking, but I wasn't sure how you would feel about it, so I didn't want to bring it up."

The benefit of having someone in your life who thinks like Tessa is that you can say pretty much anything to them and they will not be shocked. I told her what I had been scared to say aloud to anybody else, a theory I had about our mother, who had died three years earlier of emphysema, terminal anxiety, and depression. "What if Mum put this thing in me from the Great Beyond, to hook me because she's lonely? Crazy, huh? Judgy, right?" I said, trying to beat her to the punch.

"I don't think it works that way," she said, but added, "but you need to dig down into that emotional work so that it's not true *on any level.*" When she said it. I knew she was right. I was giving up my agency to a dead person.

"Would you pray for the work to be revealed to me?" I asked her. Without skipping a beat, she said, "Are you sure you really want to know?" I wondered if she knew something I didn't. I have a blessedly terrible memory, and there are things I've forgotten about our family's difficult history of addiction, mental illness, and trauma, intentionally and otherwise. But Tessa sometimes unearthed insights like an emotional archeologist.

Then, contradicting herself, she said, "You know, *I* feel partly responsible for your cancer." Years earlier, she told me, when she was recovering at my house from an abusive ex, a depressive episode, and a stint in jail for cannabis possession, she did a lot of deep meditation to get the bad karma out. I was so physically and spiritually close to her at the time, she worried that she had detoxed herself right into me, now years later where it bloomed as cancer.

Now it was my turn to say, "I don't think cancer works that way. It's not like a demon, looking for a host after it has been cast out, like what Jesus did to the Gerasene demoniac. But point taken: I'm the one thinking my dead mom is hooking me into an early grave."

I've said before that almost anything might be true once you decide to believe in God and the supernatural realm. But that doesn't mean whatever "anything" is is immutable. Powers and principalities, behind-the-scenes spiritual forces, are real. So are we. No matter what is going on, we have some agency and choices, some control over how we think about and respond to what is happening to us.

We're tempted to look for simple answers when complicated things happen, and bad theologies provide them. Consider the idea that God Has a Plan: who does that benefit, besides drugstore self-help book authors? Not to mention, this fictitious "has-a-plan" business plays suspiciously well with the status quo of hypercapitalism, patriarchy, and structural racism. It revokes our free will and our capacity to resist and change by saying that whatever is is the way things ought to be.

Take a memo, God: "Planning" is not a good look for You. Plans are rigid and we've established that You are not the rigid, uncompromising architect of our futures. You established that from the very beginning when you gave your creatures choices in the garden of Eden.

If anything, God is a Dreamer: amorphous, artistic, delighted, inclusive, and messy. God has a dream of a world where love rules, where everyone belongs, where we are more than the sum of our parts because of how we've decided to fit everyone in and the decisions we have made to love. In this fusion world, we can release enormous amounts of energy and possibility.

God also has a nightmare: eight billion individual dreams that are ego-driven and self-involved. Evil is not located in one person, but when individuals vie together against the collective to exclude, hoard, dominate, and destroy, that is God's nightmare. Theologians call it structural or social sin, and its sneakiness lies in the fact that it is often invisible. By design. The Powers That Be built our toxic systems this way, and then marketed fiction to us so we would feel individually responsible for the suffering that ensues.

Take, for example, that tear-jerking PSA from the seventies about "Keeping America Beautiful," in which a noble Indigenous man on a horse surveys the horrors of his once-pristine home degraded by litter and sheds a single, devastating tear? It turns out that commercial was funded by Coca-Cola and PepsiCo, two of the single biggest polluters. They were scapegoating us, the end users, so they could keep profiting off of pollution they created (and by the way, that Native American actor was, in fact, Italian).

So many of us have been taught, or absorbed from the ether, the idea that sin is individual. If we just work hard enough and strive to please God, we will be rewarded with an E-Z Pass through the pearly gates. Even in modern America, too many people still believe that illness, disability, or poverty are proof of God's judgment for individual sin.

But most sin, like pollution, is social and structural. It is the poison embedded in deeply complex systems, and those who benefit from those systems say they can't be changed or they will all fall apart.

If we're honest with ourselves, the idea that God has a plan is immensely comforting. It means that "God's got this." It means that whatever scary shit we go through in life, in some sense, it's all a kiddie ride, like those antique cars we thought we were really driving around at the amusement park. We can't screw up; we just have to surrender to the course God set for us.

Even garden-variety mainline Christians truck in a kind of laissez-faire fundamentalism that says "God has a plan," as if that settles that. It's intellectually and spiritually lazy.

Why would you even *want* God to have a plan? If God has a plan for you and you manage to fulfill it by the end of your life, great! You climbed the pole and rang the bell, who cares? Or you didn't fulfill it and you're an abject failure. Or you sort of fulfilled it, and that's arguably the worst outcome of all for the achievers out there (Enneagram 3s, you feeling me?).

We love to read the scripture where the Lord declares to the young prophet Jeremiah, "For I know the plans I have for you. Plans to prosper you and not to harm you, plans to give you hope and a future."

This is where if I could edit God a little bit, I would have encouraged God to say instead, "I know the *dreams* I have for you."

God lives in all times and knows the future because God has already gotten there. For those in the sciences, you could say God knows the *futures*, multiple, because string theory suggests a universe of infinite possibilities, which is more consistent with a God who created us out of a sense of adventure and longing for companionship, was immediately delighted, and called us good, and then set us free to make choices and keep becoming.

Time is nothing to God, but that doesn't mean the future is fanfiction already authored by God about Her characters. We all contain multitudes, and I expect God is more curious than judgmental about what will happen next (while at the same time knowing exactly what will happen. I know. It's a mindfuck).

The closest I've come to a sensible understanding about how God's agency squares with our agency comes from a beautiful novel by Haven Kimmel, *The Solace of Leaving Early*. In it, the protagonist, a parish minister, tries to find the language to understand this all. What he lands on is God as Lure, a great electromagnet at the heart of Creation and thrumming within our own stubborn hearts:

> *God is helpless. We are at the mercy of our own radical freedom, and all God can do is take into God's self the grief, the violence, the sublime acts of kindness, the good sex. God comes to us from the future, and has only one godlike gift: the lure. We are lured toward truth, beauty, goodness...the lure is pulling at our hearts like some lucid joy inside every actual occasion and all we have to do is...Say yes.*

God as Lure is the God I need. And the lure is reciprocal and ongoing.

As Rumi put it even more succinctly, "The longing for God *is* God." Or Aslan the lion said to Jill, "You would not have called to me unless I had been calling to you."

I Corinthians says, "Now we see through a glass, dimly, then we will see face to face. Then we will know fully, even as we are fully known." Life is an ongoing, unfolding mystery. We scarcely know ourselves, and that is part of the adventure.

Faith requires both relinquishment of control and taking charge of the freedom God gives us that no circumstances can take away. My clergy colleague Kelly did volunteer prison ministry in college. She was moved by the simple testimony of an incarcerated woman whose faith in God had changed her life, even—especially—when she was still locked up and broke. "If I'd had any strings to pull, I'd never have discovered God's grace came with no strings attached." God is a magnet, not a puppet master.

So, if it's true that sin is social and that God is more curious than judgmental, does that mean there are no wrong turns? That we just need to buckle into our kiddie rides and go? Of course not. Love still matters. Goodness and right action still matter. Healing hurts and making amends matter. There are a lot of other lures that compete with God: greed, insecurity, desire, hunger, ambition, safety. They are all human appetites and motivations to be managed, but excess or context can make them into something monstrous.

Think about the last time you were mixed up and feeling torn by opposing impulses, desires, or feelings. Did you take time to meditate, pray, or go for a long walk by yourself, and let the Lure tell you what to do next? Whatever we are facing, we can get quiet, settle into stillness, and let ourselves be pulled toward the good and toward God.

So, what about evil? The rabbi and family systems guru Edwin Friedman said that God is not an overfunctioner. He reminds us that "God did it *tzim-tzum*," a Hebrew word related to the word for raisin: God shriveled Herself up as a way of making room for human freedom, including the freedom to do wrong. "God gave you the freedom to screw up and that's the least you can do for each other," Friedman quips.

My last summer in seminary, I was required to do chaplaincy training. I chose to work at Long Lane School, the juvenile hall in Middletown, Connecticut, where some of the twelve-to-seventeen-year-olds were there for truancy, others for murder. They were white, Black, and mostly Puerto Rican. Almost all of them were poor, their lives cast into some degree of inevitability by class, race, and other intractible circumstances of birth.

Many of the kids I spoke to who were in for selling drugs told me it was the best way they knew to supplement their single mothers' incomes. None of them could really see a life for themselves other than what they knew from the neighborhood. I decided that my job was to love them, affirm the goodness I saw in them, and tell them about the God I knew, a God of curiosity and infinite second chances.

Fifteen-year-old Antonio did not live on the ward called The Unit, which was as much prison as any adult corrections facility. He stayed in one of the euphemistically named locked "cottages" that ringed the campus, with only a stern-looking guard separating him from freedom when they moved from building to building. Antonio had a four-year commitment on nonviolent drug charges (this was the nineties, the heyday of Reagan-Bush-Clinton's draconian war on drugs, which took kids prisoner for a few dumb decisions). He was 5'6" with curly brown hair and big brown eyes, and one of those god-awful caterpillar-mustaches boys in mid-puberty try desperately to grow.

On a gorgeous summer day, Antonio and three other boys were being marched single file from their cottage to the dining hall when they decided to run. They went flying through the field across the street, outrunning the huffing guards, and disappeared into the woods on the other side. Two weeks later, they were all back, and this time they were locked up in The Unit for good.

One afternoon, I went to visit Antonio. A dog-eared copy of *The Adventures of Huckleberry Finn* lay on his standard-issue gray blanket.

He told me with a light in his eyes about his hero's journey. The boys had walked most of the way from Middletown to Bridgeport, forty-three miles. They stopped to cool their feet in a fountain in the middle of some swanky Connecticut town along the way, picking loose change from the water to buy sodas on the hot day. A white lady who saw them took pity and bought them all lunch. A stranger drove them the last leg of their weary journey, no questions asked.

"It was the first real adventure I ever had," sighed Antonio.

I was stunned. In his fifteen short years, Antonio had seen more of life than most elders. He had battled the dragons of poverty, abuse, and abandonment. He had been part of the complex and fraught economy of illegal drug sales (I can't imagine what kind of emotional intelligence and courage that takes. I still feel nervous and awkward selling things on Craigslist). He was looked on by the state as a hardened criminal, but he was just a kid, looking for freedom from the chains and closed borders he was born into, craving a calling, hoping to keep becoming.

He asked me if I would bring him *The Adventures of Tom Sawyer* the next time I visited. I said, "Absolutely."

If I have any beef with God after all this time, it pretty much comes down to these three: Child sexual abuse. Chronic, unremitting mental illness. And mosquitos. All three are handicaps to living a life of unfettered joy. And yet, even facing such foes, we have agency. We have will. We have people and resources we can call upon to find freedom and healing from trauma, so we can live into God's best dreams for us.

Life puts limits on some of us more than others right out of the gate because of the circumstances of our birth. For Tessa, it's her brain chemistry and temperament. For Antonio, race and class. It is a lot to ask them to transcend when the world is wired the way that it is. Their dreaming will help them.

No matter where we walk in life, we will all meet our limits sooner or later, and we will have to look for a way out. We will need to claim all of our agency as co-dreamers with God and co-conspirators in our own futures. We will need to call on the kindness of chosen family and strangers and advocate for ourselves within unjust systems. Because many possible futures are written for each of us, and God is still dreaming.

Chapter 11

RANDOM TUESDAY DEATH WISH

I will always be a stranger who never feels at home, who does not really want and is not really wanted, who can never belong, who must always be a little in love with death!"
—*Edmund from* Long Day's Journey into Night *by Eugene O'Neill*

Sometimes I think: *It's been a good run. I'd be okay with dying.*

As a card-carrying white American female optimist, and a pastor to boot, I know the rules. I am supposed to be congenitally grateful and rosily life-embracing. I know it's a gift that I got to live through cancer, to return to the work I love, to watch my children grow up, to deepen in love and friendship, and to have new challenges, travels, and adventures. And sometimes, I want to give that gift back.

Not that I'm actively suicidal. But life is painful, and messy, and repetitive. Is it really time to brush my teeth *again*?

There were many moments during my cancer year when I worried that I had given myself cancer as a way of getting out of doing the dishes—or a way out of everything (I do overshoot the mark sometimes).

I would remember what it felt like to leave my body in the near-death-dream the night before they found the tumor, that peek into my soul's next address. I craved the freedom and peace I experienced. I still do. In the journalist Barbara Bradley Hagerty's excellent book *Fingerprints of God*, a Mexican immigrant died in a house fire, had a near-death experience of transcendent joy, and was resuscitated by paramedics. Years later, he told her, "When I think about death, I think about how nice it is to be alive and to be with my family. At the same time, I don't worry about what's going to happen later. Everything will fix itself." Here is good, but so is There.

Maybe you, like me, also sometimes flirt with the desire to beat God (or cancer, or a car wreck, or old age, or a racist cop) to the punch: to take matters into your own hands and take the guesswork out of when you will die.

As I blogged my way through cancer, it was socially acceptable to talk about my reckoning with death, my doubts about life Beyond. A pastor struggling with fear and doubt! I was an inspiration, man.

What felt impossible to talk about, the private bruise I had to keep covered, was my reckoning with life, and more particularly the banality of living, the intermittent secret flirtation with death that would intrude on my thoughts and make me want to flush all my supplements down the toilet.

I was a young mother, wife, sister, friend, and pastor. It was irresponsible of me to have these feelings, so I mostly kept them to myself. I certainly never told my husband, who was working so hard to keep me alive, because it would have been ungrateful and caused him unnecessary pain.

But as a pastor, I know how often people think about dying. They press that bruise, turning the idea over and over in their minds or just alight on it before flitting away, having terrified themselves. My friend Sarah Lund is a pastor, author, and mental health advocate. She says that people suicidally ideate much more than we imagine. We hide it from each other, and even from ourselves. She wants us to destigmatize it and normalize it.

Talking about the fact of death and the agenda we have around it isn't giving people permission to stop treatment when it's working or take their own lives. It does, however, give us a good look at the shadow, shed light on it, find the edges of the mystery.

And counterintuitively, giving ourselves permission to follow that thought-train, or having the conversation out loud with a trusted person, can help us recommit to the idea that life is really quite extraordinary. We can become more curious about what's going to happen next, even if it's more tooth-brushing. Clean teeth *do* feel amazing.

Normalizing talk about suicidal ideation also gives us an opportunity to get better prophylactic mental health treatment, and it is the best thing we can do to reduce the number of completed suicides. The second-best thing we can do is reduce the number of guns and ease of availability. Unlike most Democrats (whatever the right-wingers say), I actually *do* want to take your guns away. But I also want to make unlimited mental health care a part of every health insurance plan. Which should also include free emergency chocolate, IMHO.

My own theology of suicide has evolved a lot over the years of walking with people through treatment-resistant depression, bipolar disorder, and degenerative disease. When I was a baby minister, I thought everyone should live as long as possible and fight as hard as possible to live, no matter what they were suffering through.

At my church on the North Shore, I became close to a young woman who spent the better part of a year in a psychiatric hospital for suicidal depression. Rhoda was smart and funny, and that made it easy to pay her frequent visits. I admit I also had some ego-investment in keeping her alive. I would say things to her like, "How do you know that if you kill yourself, you won't just have to deal with the same shit on the other side? You might still have to do The Work. Why not just stay here?"

I fully, and with an appropriate amount of shame, now admit that that theology did not come from the Bible but from my imaginative watching of the movie *What Dreams May Come*, where a bereft Marisa Tomei takes her own life and finds herself in hell. Not that I believed in hell, even then. However (like a good Protestant), I did believe in work. My intentions were good, but what a terrible thing to say to someone just looking for relief. My friend Ellen, a psychologist, says, "Suicidal ideation is as much a wish for rest as it is a wish for death. It's a wish for relief—so overwhelming that a person is willing to consider accepting the permanence of dying."

Losing Gary helped me grow up as a pastor to people struggling with the lure of suicidal rest. Gary and his husband, Marlin, were temperamentally opposites: Gary was small and slim, quiet, and artistic. Marlin was larger than life with a booming laugh, commanding every room he entered, quick with a joke, and always ready to party. Marlin never did anything by half-measures and had a huge appetite for life that had won him great personal and professional success, but also periodically included cocaine binges, during which he'd lose everything and have to start from scratch.

When he came to our church, he was five years married to Gary, the love of his life, and six months sober. Marlin and his whirlwind energy were a huge boon to our tiny but growing church and also helped us expand into our mission and purpose as a sanctuary for other folks working the Twelve Steps. I often said that our best spiritual teachers in the congregation were the addicts in recovery because they taught us by example all about resurrection, grace, and how to be a people for others.

I didn't know Gary as well as Marlin, partly because he stayed in Marlin's shadow, sitting quietly in the fifth pew while Marlin belted out a vigorous tenor from the choir loft. Whether his retiring nature was by temperament or a function of the depression, I don't know because I never got to meet Gary fully unencumbered by poor mental health. But as the years passed, particularly during one really terrible two-year stint of treatment-resistant depression involving multiple hospitalizations, we grew closer, and I got to know his wry sense of humor, his sweetness, and his longings.

On her fifth birthday, as I had just finished chemo, Gary gave Carmen an original copy of the bleakly wonderful children's book *Fortunately/ Unfortunately*, in which the hero embarks on a series of adventures that are an ouroboros of tragedy and salvation. You could say he was preparing Carmen for life, Gary-style.

Gary had more spiritual doubts than Marlin. While I would try to get him curious about the Fortunately that was certain to follow the current Unfortunately if only he could wait it out, it was hard for him to see past the current desolation. He submitted to multiple rounds of electroshock therapy, meant to rewire the depressive brain. Instead, for Gary, it put him into cardiac arrest and he had to be paddled back to life. I remember being cautiously hopeful that when his heart stopped, he might have seen The Light and heard a voice telling him to go back and live a long and beautiful earthly life. But he remembered nothing, even admitting to some despair that they had brought him back.

During month two of a hospitalization at McLean Hospital in Belmont, he asked me if I believed he would go to hell if he took his own life. Then and there, I realized I believed that a good God could not possibly permit Their own child, who was suffering so much in life, to suffer one moment longer in death.

"I want to be careful how I say this," I said, "because suicide leaves a terrible exit wound. You are SO loved here, even if you can't always feel it. Marlin loves you so much and you know it would profoundly destabilize him if you died. No matter what you say, you are not *ever* a burden to him. And I love you so much and you have a brother and parents and a church full of people who need you here. That said, if you were to die, I believe God would open Her arms wide to you, and give you rest from your pain."

Gary left as small an exit wound as he could manage. There was no blood, no traumatizing image of a dangling body etched in the hippocampus of his beloveds for the rest of their lives. He mail-ordered a cocktail of drugs he knew would kill him, left a note on the front door for his husband that said, "Call the police, then call Molly," then quietly ended his life, on the bed, with his two beloved Welsh corgis keeping vigil.

That Monday morning, Marlin had a funny feeling and went home to check on Gary at lunchtime. I rushed over after Marlin called me. He was keening and wailing on the front lawn of his house while neighbors walked their dogs and toddlers. I went into the house, upstairs. Gary was lying there, his face in deep repose. I was able to tell Marlin, honestly, that I felt Gary was released from his long suffering, and at peace.

What may bring one person peace can leave others devastated. Deaths—suicides, chief among them—always have repercussions for the living. It always feels like there's more we could have and should have done. For those who worry "how could my loved one have been suffering so much, and I didn't know?" the phase of acute distress that precedes a suicide attempt, completed or not, is often intense but very brief. It doesn't give lie to the apparent happiness and pleasurable moments they experienced before the devastating event.

But in Gary's case, the impulse was chronic and not acute. For months, Marlin had been getting Gary out of bed and bringing him to work with him, keeping him on personal suicide watch. But even Marlin, with his big, structural, can-do entrepreneur energy, couldn't lift the weight off of Gary.

After Gary's death, Marlin had two separate relapses into addiction, losing everything all over again before he found his way back. He began back at Step 1. He spent a year as director of a national organization that helps families who love someone with depression. He has loved again, though never the way he loved Gary. He eventually moved to the small town where he first got sober, found a big job there, volunteers at the rehab with folks newly in recovery, and is happy today with two new corgi puppies, having in subsequent years buried both of their older dogs.

On the seventh anniversary of Gary's death, Marlin wrote this:

> *Seven years. Seven years since my beloved husband left this world too soon because he just couldn't take the depression one more day. That day in 2014 will always be the 'before' and 'after' point for my life.*
>
> *Grief is a strange and wondrous thing. It exists only when you have great love. It remains because you continue to remember that love. But it does indeed change as the years pass. Today I remember much less the way that Gary died and much more the life he lived. The life we lived together.*
>
> *Seven years ago, grief lied to me and told me my future died with Gary on May 5, 2014. That wasn't true. Today, seven years 'after' I have a life that I didn't plan to have, but is nonetheless fulfilling and love-filled. Today I have two dogs that Gary never met, live in a house he never visited, and live in a town he knew, but didn't really know at all.*

This year I had the opportunity to share my experience with suicide and grief with another family who lost someone they loved very much. I was able to take my experience from seven years ago to understand their pain, their grief, their anger. Everything I experienced and went through led me to the moment seven years later where I could provide just a bit of comfort, a glimmer of understanding, and perhaps some hope to someone else just starting their journey through grief. Thank you, Gary, for being my love and for giving me the part of your life that you did. For that, I will be forever grateful.

For years, for Marlin's sake, Gary tried to stay. He really tried. But he couldn't. He'd done his time in hell. And finally, God loved him and welcomed him On.

Not everyone can accept this perspective on suicide. When I told one of my parishioners about my conversation with Gary, and my belief that God awaits us all with welcome, he was furious with me. He left the church and sent me a long single-spaced letter that ended, "You have failed me as a pastor."

Our society, as a whole, fears death and avoids it. The intrusiveness of neck cream ads on my Facebook feed underscores this, as does the edginess of some of my recently-retired church members who don't quite know what to do with themselves now that their career is over, but who are nowhere near ready to die.

But facing death is ultimately what frees us to live more wholly. That is what so many of our wisdom traditions teach us, from Jesus facing death head-on to the Buddhist "corpse meditation" that asks us to contemplate our own maggot-ridden decomposing bodies (yum!) as an advanced lesson in being human.

My second hospitalization, late in cancer treatment, came as a surprise. I had been feeling great. My convos with Nurse Kerry during infusion were less about pain and symptom management and more like parental bitch sessions between friends and a chance to try out new stand-up material. My chemo cocktails were getting lighter and leaner, and with bestie Sue, as Christmas approached, I wrote a ditty at my twelfth round of chemo:

On the twelfth round of chemo, my cancer gave to me
Twelve prunes for peristalsis
Eleven moiling mouth sores
Ten fingers failing
Nine needle stickings
Eight torrid hot flashes
Seven nights no napping
Six queasy car rides
Five golden nurses!
Four fevers flaring
Three wigs a wearing
Two children caring
And a painted pair of perfect eyebrows!

But a few days after the cocktail finished, I was shaking with fever without even two white blood cells to knock together. It was December 21, and as they wheeled me from Dana Farber Cancer Institute through the glass walkway to Brigham and Women's Hospital across the street for admission, I heard the strains of a string quartet floating cheerfully back at me, "Have Yourself a Merry Little Christmas."

I was desperate to get home in time for Christmas, to hear that song play unironically while snuggled on the sofa with my family nestled around me. At the same time, I was acutely aware of the reality of Christ's birth amid struggle and chills and humility and discomfort and the clanging threat of mortality. Love born into the world in spite of, and not because of, every good thing lining up.

Even with the last seventeen episodes of *Sex and The City* downloaded on my iPad, all I could muster the energy to do was stare at the wall and wait. A long, dark Advent waiting.

This time, the children did not visit. I was worn down by Adriamycin, the Red Devil, by all the devils, who it suddenly seemed to me were winning.

I could not find my brave face for them. I felt acutely that my life was hanging by a thread as thin as the bird necklace gracing my neck, and death might be a relief. Sue, however, braved cross-Boston traffic to come and walk me up and down the halls of the Brigham, every single day. She walked me back to life.

On the fourth day, Christmas Eve, my blood counts began to rebound, and I was safe to go home. That evening, I sat in the back pew at church wearing a hospital mask because I was still so vulnerable to infection.

But there was no masking my tears. I oohed with all the others at a five-day-old Baby Jesus on the chancel, tender new life that had found a way through the gauntlet of death. I sang "Silent Night" through blue polypropylene and wondered how I could ever have entertained thoughts of leaving this party early.

When my time does come, I'm ready, liturgically speaking. My funeral plans live in a folder on my Mac. I made them long before cancer happened, motivated by garden-variety creative control issues. I have done a lot of funerals, and among them, a number of boring and bad ones. I didn't want to leave my funeral plans to a disoriented, grief-stricken husband and a panicked community of friends and parishioners.

When somebody we love dies, even when the deceased was old or death anticipated, often the funeral prep still seems to happen in a rush and fit into the Traditional Protestant Funeral Box: Three hymns on pipe organ (that is, if people are even willing to sing), one of two cliché scriptures, one-size-fits-all prayers. We honor a ninety-three-year life with a twenty-eight-minute service, and follow it with flavorless Crisco-based supermarket pastries and bad coffee in the parish hall.

I hate to say it, but my religious tradition doesn't do funerals and memorial services well. WASPs are notoriously shy of emoting, and we've never dealt adequately with our fear of death. When it's my turn, give me a Mexican or Haitian three-day festival, and go ahead and throw in some hired mourners, a case of bubbly, and a dance party. And you better CRY, or I will come back and haunt you.

Still, every once in a while, we Frozen Chosen get it right. When Virginia, a beloved elder in our church died, per her wishes we sang "In the Garden" upstairs in the sanctuary and wept, then went downstairs to the parish hall to dance to Elton John's "Crocodile Rock" while laughing our heads off. That is the kind of funeral I hope to have. (See, funeral planning is not morbid. It's just good, sensible egomania.)

Funerals are also catharsis for the grieving. Have you ever been to a funeral where you didn't recognize the person you were memorializing, not in one word that was said or sung? We work overtime painting them as a saint, erasing the frailties and flaws and regrets and mistakes and all the things that made them THEM, and then we are surprised when our grief moves in and overstays its welcome like a bad roommate who doesn't pay the rent and leaves a mess.

And yet, this is what our rites and rituals are designed for. My colleague Wendy says that through our liturgy we rehearse life. Liturgy can help us metabolize big feelings and transitions, including the "good goodbye" we all need when someone moves on, either to the other side of the country, or the other side of the veil.

In spite of my freewheeling "Wounded Healer/there's a crack in everything, it's how the light gets in" theology, sometimes even I can't see the beauty in the brokenness. Bits, pieces, flotsam, jetsam, shards that can't easily be mended or repurposed annoy the shit out of me.

I am a compulsive neatnik, and I don't like things that don't have a tidy place. Illness, chronic illness, terminal illness especially, make for a lot of flotsam and jetsam. It is a whole lot of mess. There are a lot of things that don't 'fit.'

My job as a human, even if I don't like it, is just to *live* each messy, imperfect day, not rushing either life or death. And "living each day" doesn't always mean focusing on joy or accentuating the positive. Sometimes it means just getting the meds right, making sure I eat something healthy, and breathing, all day long. And, usually, brushing my teeth.

—

When I was in the bargaining phase of my cancer-grief, I went to God and said, "I don't need a super-long life. I'd be happy to get to an independent, vigorous seventy-eight, or even seventy-two. I'd like to see my kids grow up, meet their spouses if they marry, know their children if they have any, for a little while. And none of this sneaking in a chronic illness. If I'm not going to live to be very old, I want to LIVE until I die."

This, of course, is not a prayer I imagine works the way God works. But it doesn't hurt, again, to start by praying for what you really want.

In thinking about my ideal death age, though, I had to wonder about my choice—why seventy-two? I've known a lot of old people, and *really* old people, in my life. It comes with the job. Some have lived cheerfully and well, without too much physical discomfort, until the moment of their deaths. Some have lived cheerfully and well even *with* physical discomfort.

I've also known old folks who seem so unhappy, so diminished in their own eyes, so unable or unwilling to enjoy the pleasures that are still available to them, deeply hung up on past mistakes, or wrongs done to them, or broken relationships.

Even though I want to say, "I wouldn't be like them," I really can't be sure.

I always wonder why people have such a hard time adjusting to life in assisted livings and nursing homes. Yes, they can be smelly, undignified, loud, even cruel places, but there are pleasures to be had. On perfect spring days, so many who still have their bodily autonomy stay in their room with the TV blaring rather than going out to smell the roses.

On second thought: the elderly Californians I know, who all seem to come fragranced with fresh lavender and still hike the chaparral-dotted hills well into senescence, seem to enjoy their old age more than other seniors I've known. There is Lenore, who walks in the rooftop garden of her retirement community and prays for the world; and Lewis, who took up poetry in his nineties after being twice widowed; and Martin, who sometimes escapes his room to sit in the lobby, saying, "I snuck out of jail!" like a mischievous kindergartner.

There is Myrna, who hiked out of the Sierras alone after her husband had an aneurysm at the high camp and there wasn't room for her in the helicopter. She did clown ministry for the youth group into old age. While she was suffering through a terribly painful case of shingles in her optic nerve, she told me that even though she couldn't be on my pastor-parish relations committee anymore, I was welcome to come and fling myself on her bed and cry whenever I wanted. So, I guess, if you can, get old in California.

Then again, even among the hardened New Englanders, there were sunny spirits, like Edith. She was legally blind, and pretty out of it mentally in her later years, but she remains one of my Gold Standards for Getting Old people. When I arrived to visit, she always had her face in the sun, sitting in a rocking chair in front of her assisted living facility. She ate with gusto her breakfasts, her lunches, her dinners, but she was not a glutton. She wasn't trying to fill a hole. She loved to tell off-color jokes and swear, and she told me, on every single visit, that she was ready to go whenever God took her, but she didn't mind sticking around until that day. I never saw her crabby, not once.

And finally, there was Dibbie, one of the matriarchs of my church in Somerville. She had more than her share of tragedy and grief in her life. As a young adult, she found her mother dead on the kitchen floor of the home they shared. She lost her beloved sister Ruthie very young and mothered Ruthie's children in the aftermath. She outlived all her siblings, and many of her friends, before dying at age ninety-four. I often heard her say, though not bitterly, that she didn't know why God kept her around. She was just curious about it. She told me once that she thought eighty-three was the perfect age to die. She was ninety-two at the time. But she persisted.

While she was waiting for God to take her home, she continued driving her remaining friends to lunch and church, making ceramics, and helping with the community meal for the homeless, something she did every single week without a break for thirty years until she decided to cut herself some slack at age eighty-seven. She got up early to pray, never missed a Pats game, and found divine relief in cussing at the bad ref calls.

She was grateful for all of it, especially the independence she had until nearly the end. She knew how good she had it. But I couldn't help but believe she invited this goodness, following God's lure and receiving grace because of how she prioritized her life and energy.

Others, like Jenny Utech, died entirely too soon and against all of our wishes, including hers, though she went graciously at the end. Jenny was one of the most big-hearted, sensible, and hardworking Christians I knew. She spent her weekdays working for Partners in Health, the same organization that brought Junior to the States to save his life, and gave her weekends quietly and without fanfare toward making our church come alive again.

Rev. Day, the drag gospel preacher who became the new pastor of Somerville when I moved to California, called to tell me that the ovarian cancer Jenny kept quiet for years was finally besting her, and invited me to pray with Jenny on the phone. I sobbed in my car on the way to work. *Not Jenny. Jenny's not the one, God.*

The next morning, I again got on the phone to speak with Jenny, and though she was unconscious, her mother and sister held the phone up to her ear, and this is what I said:

> *"I have so much to say, but don't want to make the mistake that so many ministers make which is talking too much*
> > *"How often I've thought about you*
> > *What a deeply good person you are, Jenny*
> > *Stubbornly loyal; the fierceness and clarity of your moral compass.*
> > *I can still hear your voice in nearly all of our congregational meetings over the years, as we're circling and circling and trying to get*

the plane to land and you, usually standing at the edge of the room, suddenly say with your sense of urgency, "You guys, here's the thing," and you say the thing, and it suddenly all becomes so clear to us, what God wants and needs us to do and how possible it all is

I think about how when you first came to First Church you said, "Is this a loser church?" because there weren't that many people there yet, and you decided to become one of the losers anyhow

And everything we built, was so much because of you

Your willingness to show up

To do what needed to be done

Whatever it was—from dishes to deaconing to holding babies so parents could get a break

The best hander-outer at the Christmas and Easter outreach tables, because no one could say no to you. I still teach your technique—that no-nonsense, kind-and-not-weird literal outreach from one human to another, calling people into community

Last night I looked at a picture of you holding baby Izzy in the nursery

You didn't raise children of your own but you were a good auntie to so many kids who needed you

I also saw Junior last week

He's thriving. He's a miracle. I think of how many people you've helped find a new life, Jenny, how many lives you have had a hand in saving

But you are so much more than the things you have done

You are just Good through and through

It makes me so sad to know that you are leaving this world, and too soon

A thing about that

I don't know what you believe about the afterlife

But here's what I know

The night before my totally accidental and random cancer diagnosis came in, I had a dream…

And the dream was not a dream but a visitation of God, an experience of what happens when we are liberated from our bodies

And Jenny, we're not nothing

We're the opposite of nothing

We are Everything

I hope this brings you some peace and some comfort

And I know in your way you are probably facing this new adventure with the same calm determination that you face everything

One last thing

My first memory of you

We were at Bruegger's Bagels in Porter Square. I was still new at our church and wanted to take everybody out for coffee and learn their story

And what I most remember is, Rafe was two and oppositional and we were struggling to understand how to parent him

And you said something like "If you just love your kids, really love them, it's enough" and you cried a little as you said it, Holy Spirit tears

And I never forgot it

And we have had a couple of really hard years with Rafe, ironically as I was writing a book with Ellen purporting to be a Parenting Expert

And one of the closing lines is really, basically your parenting advice

And you know what? It's TRUE

Peter and I both really love Rafe and he really loves us back and we say it every day. He never leaves the house without saying it to us, and we're not quite done with the troubles I don't think, but it is enough

And I love YOU so much, like a mother and daughter and sister in one
And I miss you
But Jesus knows the place where you are going and He has prepared a place for you
You're going from Love to Love
And I'm praying right now
For you to land softly into the next Love.
And also for this moment, if you can, for you to be able to open your eyes while you are still here, and see the Love that is staring you in the face

One very good reason to stick around as long as possible is that this world is so frigging beautiful. In a small vase next to my laptop is a peony so amazing in its louche perfection that my heart just skipped a beat looking at it. Outside my window, I can hear the crows teasing the cooper's hawk, and the cooper's hawk giving it right back.

And in a minute when I close the lid on this chapter, my now fifteen-year-old daughter, not too leggy for cuddles, will probably crawl in my lap and tell me all about her first day of in-person high school because the pandemic has entered a more liberated chapter. Frigging beautiful.

And if life is not always frigging beautiful, we can count on it to be weird and full of surprises. Who even knows what will happen next?

Chapter 12

LOSERS FOR JESUS

My husband is, at the moment, searching madly for his wedding ring. "I *just* had it on this morning!" he says in an anxious voice. During the pandemic, he got out of the habit of wearing it, but he has a presentation with the CEO of his company over Zoom this afternoon.

"I guess you want to signal to the higher-ups that you are someone other people can tolerate living with?" I say wryly before joining him in the hunt since I wasn't getting any writing done with him flapping around the bedroom.

I find the ring on my side of the sink, camouflaged by the fake granite countertop. "Now calm the fuck down," I say playfully. Adding, "It's an important thing, but it's just a thing." Then I give him a long hug.

The poet Elizabeth Bishop wrote about the art of losing: "It isn't hard to master—so many things seem filled with the intent to be lost that their loss is no disaster." Losing is a part of life, and a way of making space for the things, people, practices, values, and realities more necessary to the moment.

Jesus said in the Gospels, "Those who want to save their life will lose it, and those who lose their life for my sake, and the sake of the gospel, will save it. What does it profit to gain the whole world but forfeit your life?"

This might be a straight-up call to martyrdom. But I think we are worth a lot more to the Way of Jesus by taking it metaphorically as a call to a life of service rather than a premature heroic death. It's a shorthand for getting over our egos and disordered desires, the spiritual practice of letting go and welcoming our status as "losers for Jesus."

To become good losers means we acknowledge, at some level, that a rich and meaningful life is born as much by subtraction as it is by addition, by what is taken away from us and how we make meaning in the aftermath, as it is by life's gifts and blessings.

Even those events generally acknowledged as positive—the birth of a child, a new job, a call to the ministry—rob us of freedom and time, stress our relationships, and demand sacrifices.

Cancer, or any intense physical experience like it, takes a lot away from us. It's not all resurrection and roses. There are lingering physical effects, cognitive diminishment. The growth machine of hypercapitalism, in which there is never anywhere to go but up, is not mirrored in our physical lives.

The reality Carl Jung named a long time ago is this: we are born. Our lives, capacities, skills, and spheres of influence grow and expand. We learn how to stop pooping and peeing ourselves, which opens up a lot more possibilities. We make friends—some of us, quite a lot of friends. We learn to walk, drive, even fly. Someday we may learn how to run a committee meeting, write a book, bake a perfect loaf of sourdough, grow a garden, or start a company.

We impact our neighbors, coworkers, and family with new ideas and infectious action. Some of us even become famous and have enormous influence over culture or public policy: changing the course of climate change, or ushering in the resurrection of shoulder pads. What we do has a visible, palpable ripple effect on the world around us.

But at some point, our lives start to contract. Our energies diminish. Our eyesight grows dim. Once old, we become young again: dribbling our food out of messy mouths, wearing adult diapers, becoming nonverbal, the ranks of our friends thinning as one by one our contemporaries pass out of this life before us. Addiction might get its claws into us and refuse to be shaken loose. We may run out of money before we run out of years. We turn inward, and sometimes our spirits begin to leave this mortal coil well before our bodies do.

The loss of who we believe ourselves to be, which happens not once but over and over again, is extremely painful.

One of my parishioners, facing a new breast cancer diagnosis, said: "I don't care if I lose my boobs—but what if I lose myself because of having to give up hormone replacement therapy? I don't like the irritable, drained, unfocused me—that is not who I am, but that is who I have been over the past few days. I don't usually pray. I do believe 'thy will be done' and it is what it will be, and there isn't some Person in the Sky that is listening to me ask for a specific outcome or request. And if there isn't, what is the point [in praying] other than 'centering' in the way meditation would?"

A doctor, she is pragmatic. Who among us can expect immortality? Life will take things and people away from us, one at a time, and sometimes all at once.

As we diminish in body, we have the opportunity to grow in soul. It's only ego that wants to hold onto every good thing, perfectly and forever. And as Elizabeth Lesser wrote in *Broken Open*, "Would you rather be an ego or a soul?"

Serenity gains in letting go—of stuff, money, abilities, rancor, conflict, even ideas of right and wrong.

It is right to fight for some things rather than rolling over in the privileged haze of surrender to the status quo. I'm not saying we shouldn't fight, particularly for vulnerable people, creatures, and the earth itself. We are morally obligated to fight for justice, equality, and transformation from our culture's death-dealing ways.

But part of this fight is surrender, particularly for those of us who have been deeply trained in the ways of striving, competing, hoarding, and protecting this-worldly goods. Letting go—of our personal privileges, profit, and power—is a different kind of fight, and a deep spiritual benefit.

We can actively cultivate our own powerlessness, to understand and approach life "from below," in empathy and solidarity with powerless people, as Leonardo Boff and other liberation theologians have taught. Freeing others, we free ourselves.

When Amber called me for the first time, having found our church in Somerville online, I could hardly hear her, she spoke so haltingly and quietly. She had already taken the most difficult and dangerous step: leaving her abusive husband, her job as an elementary schoolteacher, and her home in the suburbs. She was safe at the women's shelter in my town. But now in the quiet, she was wrestling with the religious implications of what she had done. "Will God be angry with me that I left my marriage? That I'm divorcing?"

I took a breath and prayed for the Holy Spirit to send me the words. "Your marriage ended the first time he hurt you," I answered. "You didn't end the marriage. He did."

A few days later, on Sunday, Amber came to church, sitting alone in a back pew, too scared and shy to talk to anyone. She stayed at the edge of coffee hour, waiting patiently for me, and together we walked down to Davis Square in the sunshine of a perfect fall day.

It was warm enough to sit outside, and though she was visibly shaking because she was out in public, so exposed, she kept saying over and over, "I can't believe I'm just sitting here having tea with a pastor," like a lifer sprung from solitary confinement into the bright light of freedom.

Amber became a regular at church over the next few weeks. She came to our All-Church Workday and spent hours in the nursery sanitizing toys with a lovely man who'd been sexually abused as a child. Neither one had children of their own, but both sat there in service to our church children, healing. She found a minimum-wage job to pay the bills and began to think about moving in with another woman from the shelter and her son.

Then she discovered that her husband had leased an apartment just a few blocks from the church. He had somehow figured out what city she was in and was looking for her with intent to kill this time, she was sure.

She met with her social workers and with me. We agreed that she was in grave danger. She needed a new plan, and fast. Something akin to entering a witness protection program, changed name and all.

The church and DV agency provided her with startup funds to make a new life somewhere else. She picked a place she had never been, but always dreamed of. It turned out I had a pastor friend there with a marvelous church, who invited her to stay with him and his family while she got on her feet.

They grew close, and when she moved out to an apartment of her own, his girls cried. My pastor friend told me, "God is good, as they say. She has become a blessing in our world as much as we've aided in her new life."

The following spring, she recorded this testimony that we played on Easter Sunday about her own resurrection:

Now is the time when we bring our own stories before God.

I didn't really want to be resurrected. To be resurrected you have to die, to lose your life to find God. And I was not going to volunteer for that. I liked my house in a cute little town, my husband, my four-minute commute to my dream job, and my weekly farm share of organic produce.

But I had a problem: I lived my life in a constant state of fear. I was terrified of stirring the coffee the wrong way or forgetting to include a spoon in my husband's lunch bag because I knew the consequences of "disobedience" were dire. I sometimes wonder what the neighbors thought when they saw me sobbing hysterically at 10 p.m. on a Tuesday night as I futilely tried to scrub an oil stain out of the driveway.

And so, one summer morning, I woke up at the usual time, did a load of laundry, cleaned the bathroom, and kissed my husband goodbye. I said I was going to work and that was the last time I saw my home and my belongings.

You know that nervous feeling when you leave the house and wonder if you have forgotten to lock the door or turn off the stove? I have that sometimes and then I realize that yes, I did forget something. I forgot everything. And then I remember that I didn't accidentally leave it all behind, but that to save my life, I had to lose it.

As a child, I always thought of Easter as a completely happy holiday. It was all about new and eternal life. But I never really thought about the suffering and loss that made the resurrection possible.

Now I have lived it. I miss everything: my town, my colleagues, my name, and my dry cleaner. No one knows what happened to me. Even my family doesn't know where I live now. Everything that I thought defined me was suddenly gone.

But then something wonderful happened. God was EVERYWHERE. I found Him in the faces of the professionals who helped me escape. He was in the pews of this church, when I sat shaking in the back row and Molly prayed with me. God was in the kindness of new friends and a police officer who is never too busy to talk. God even stopped by the Cambridgeside Galleria, when a twenty-one-year-old Apple store employee spent two hours making my laptop safe.

He was there my third day in shelter, when I finally had an appetite, but was still too scared to venture outside for groceries. I rummaged through the cabinet, which was unusually empty that week, and could only come up with matzo that had been donated after Passover and mini packs of mustard from Panera. As I stood at the sink enjoying my gourmet and inadvertently biblical snack, I breathed deeply for the first time in years.

I felt the sweet peace of freedom and knew I was not alone.

Resurrection has not been easy. I am far from home and get lost everywhere I go. I walk six miles a day to work and make just over minimum wage. But now I live in a world filled with simple pleasures, like eating cheese for dinner and watching Netflix in bed, without fear of reprimand or punishment.

I have found the joy that comes with losing everything and finding myself nothing but a child of God.

Amber and I stayed in touch, even after I moved to Berkeley. A year or so later, she sent me this note:

My life has never been better. It's like God said no to so many of the things I desperately wanted, but what He gave me is more and better than I ever could have imagined.

I still have nightmares a lot…But most things are really wonderful. It is crazy how much things have changed since that day I first met you for tea in Somerville.

In the note, she sent photos, one with the new tattoo on her wrist that says, "be brave," and a little bird flying out of a cage next to it.

When Jesus rises from the dead, it is not as an oiled, brawny superhero or some kind of gorgeous self-healing immortal vampire. He rises with his wounds, the sign of what he has lost, of what the fullness of life and commitment to this Way has cost him.

Henri Nouwen, the priest who became depressed in Bolivia and found healing in the company of children, wrote, "Nobody escapes being wounded. We all are wounded people, whether physically, emotionally, mentally, or spiritually. The main question is not 'How can we hide our wounds?' so we don't have to be embarrassed, but 'How can we put our woundedness in the service of others?' When our wounds cease to be a source of shame, and become a source of healing, we have become wounded healers."

After a crisis, a trauma, a terrible chapter of living, we all want to go back to normal. But there's no going back. We have scars, we have active wounds, and we have a trauma response. We also have strength, resiliency, and know-how that got us through—know-how we can keep to ourselves, or share with others to help them find a way.

A lot of the new research into trauma gives us concrete ways to be participants in our own healing, and almost all of those practices are a group effort. In *What Happened to You?*, Oprah and Dr. Bruce Perry cite four major ways that humans since our earliest civilizations have metabolized trauma: (1) connection to tribe, (2) co-regulation through rhythm such as in dance or drumming, (3) storytelling and meaning-making, and (4) occasionally, through judicious use of psychedelic substances for healing in guided communal religious rituals.

The Twelfth Step of AA sums up this orientation to service after suffering "Having had a spiritual awakening as the result of these steps, we tried to carry this message to alcoholics, and to practice these principles in all our affairs."

The summer I was in chemo, my baby sister Emily got sober. Even during the worst of her addiction, Emily, pragmatic and strong-willed, functioned better than most humans, so we missed the signs for a long time. But we did notice her increasingly erratic behavior, absence from our lives, lack of communication, and a new tic: borrowing money.

I asked her to come with me to my second opinion with an oncologist at Mass General in May, right after diagnosis, because I needed someone clear-headed both to drive me and ask questions of the doctor. It also meant she was trapped alone in a car with me for forty-five minutes in Storrow Drive traffic, and I could grill her about what was really going on.

She came clean that she was using, sometimes more, sometimes less. She wanted to get sober, but wanted to do it on her own terms, by herself, in effect saying, "I got myself into this, and it's my responsibility to get myself out."

We talked about AA, about God and spirituality. Emily was by her own definition "allergic to church," but I invited her anyway, telling her that we had a lot of wonderful folks in recovery. She practically shivered at the thought. She thought that "hard work and family" were going to fix her addiction, the way she had fixed it a couple of times before.

I told her, "I want to support you, but I've never known anyone who successfully got clean and stayed clean without some sort of spirituality. They could do it for a while, a long while, and were proud that they'd done it, but it didn't really change the bottom line."

"But I feel so anxious when I walk into a church," she said. "That can't be it."

"Most lifelong *Christians* feel anxious walking into a church. Churches can be mean and hurtful; they can fail you because they are full of flawed people. And then, too, there's God—who might want to take everything away from you, the things you think are working that are *so* not working. God's a bastard that way."

I told her I loved her, and that I'd do whatever I could for her that would actually help without enabling.

She said, "That's what I don't like about NA and AA—one of the steps is something like, 'God will entirely remove these defects,' but *I'm* the one who removes them. I've never blamed other people or asked other people to take responsibility for my screwups."

Two months later, she called me on my birthday. I was in the depths of Chemolandia. She was at a residential rehab in the mountains, where she was guided to the Twelve Steps of Alcoholics Anonymous. It was the same rehab where Marlin from my church had recently gotten sober (God may or not be an asshole, but God is definitely a showoff).

She, who never cried in front of people if she could help it, told me through tears how she had sat in the chapel and found herself able to be quiet for the first time in a very, very long time. And she wasn't afraid.

Ten years later, she is now the director of nursing at a rehab facility, helping other people struggling with substances find their way back from the valley of the shadow of death. She is married to a good man who also works for the same community, a man with fifteen years of sobriety under his belt.

They have two young children whom they are teaching important lessons about asking for help, making mistakes, and being imperfect and human and still very much loved. In short: how to be "good losers."

I am blessed with a lot of losers for friends. My bestie Christopher was a hospice chaplain, a practicing Buddhist, and a hilarious young curmudgeon.

He died at age thirty-seven of a terrible brain cancer that strung him along for three years. During those three years, his wife, Robin, also a minister, became pregnant with their second child. His one viable sperm had successfully run the gauntlet of chemo, creating a baby he would say goodbye to when Ulysses was only six months old.

I'm sure Christopher would much rather have lived to old age (or at least to see his children graduate: his stated wish before he died) than become one of our spiritual teachers, but cancer melted away his inner cynic in ways that benefited all of us. One of my favorite memories was of seeing Christopher at Star Island, the UU/UCC church camp on an island off of Portsmouth, New Hampshire, about a year before he died. This recovering misanthrope was sporting a "free hugs" pin he would have mocked relentlessly a few years earlier.

While Christopher was actively dying, I had a miscarriage and was grieving hard. I called Robin, who said to me flat out, "Sometimes, God asks you to let go of what you want." I was a little mad at her for saying it, but she was right. I was grateful that she used her authority as a future young widow to say it boldly and unapologetically.

⸺

God doesn't make the fractures, but God will make use of them. Nothing has revealed the fractures of the world we live in quite like the pandemic. Religious and nonreligious folks alike think of apocalypse as a time of terror and cataclysmic, world-ending death. Certainly, that describes what we are enduring, those dead of COVID or climate chaos, police violence or racist hatred, deaths of despair or from hard use by the machinery of the modern economy.

A little reminder here that apocalypse literally means "revealing": the curtain pulled back on what has been hidden. More than anything, apocalypse is an opportunity to discern and to re-shape the habits and systems and relationships that run our lives.

Richard Rohr writes, "We would have done history a great favor if we would have understood apocalyptic literature. It's not meant to strike fear in us as much as a radical rearrangement. It's not the end of the world. It's the end of worlds—our worlds that we have created. In the book of Revelation (also called the Apocalypse, or Revelation to John), John is trying to describe what it feels like when everything falls apart. It's not a threat. It's an invitation to depth. It's what it takes to wake people up to the real, to the lasting, to what matters. It presents the serious reader with a great "What if?"

Most of us, once we reach adulthood, learn most reliably when experiencing grief, loss, or pain. This came home one day in September 2020, the day Bay Areans call "The Orange Day." Smoke from the worst western wildfires on record was wrecking the skies, and we woke to what felt, all day, like nuclear winter or alien invasion. It gave those of us who live here a terrifying glimpse into the future, what could happen if we did not make a wholesale change in the way we are using up the earth.

Others have described this season as a Reckoning, but that remains to be seen. It's only a reckoning if we actually reckon: if we count the cost of how we have been living, how we have been treating ourselves, one another, and the earth, how we have been using or abusing our power and privileges, and make the necessary changes toward a life of greater kin-dom: interrelatedness and mutual aid.

This has been a winnowing time, a time to hold on to the nourishing substance of how we really want to spend our limited time here with one another in this extraordinary place, while letting so much chaff fly away in the next mega-hurricane.

My colleague Kit preached a sermon on losing in late-pandemic Lent. She quoted Parker Palmer in saying that "Suffering breaks our hearts, but the heart can break in two different ways. There's the brittle heart that breaks into shards, shattering the one who suffers as it explodes, and sometimes taking others down when it's thrown like a grenade at the ostensible source of its pain. Then there's the supple heart, the one that breaks open, not apart, the one that can grow into greater capacity for the many forms of love. Only the supple heart can hold suffering in a way that opens to new life."

She asked us to lose like Jesus asked us to: to suffer in a way that makes us more supple. To let disaster write itself on our hearts in a way that alchemizes into poetry, meaning, transformation, even beauty. This is not to romanticize suffering but to lean into the stretch of it so we can keep growing.

She preached, "So next time you lose your keys, or lose your way, or look up and it's 5 p.m. and you've lost a day, or lost your cool at a loved one, or lost that very loved one, see if you can slowly give it over to God. Let it teach you, stretch you, break you open, again and again, for Love's sake."

As chemo wound down, I found myself fantasizing about getting a tattoo over my surgery scars—to disappear those signs of suffering, to paper over them with art, specifically: an image of that Holy Spirit Portal.

How did I imagine her? I saw Her as a juicy, bodacious woman effortlessly flying across my rib cage, breath coming in curlicues exhaling power, face like an angel, chased by the doves that have often stood as the Holy Spirit's earthly symbol.

By the time I finally got Her etched into my body, years later in San Francisco, I knew Her job wasn't to hide my scars, but to frame them.

Chapter 13

ON NOT MAKING EVERY MOMENT COUNT

Chemo ended with a whimper and not a bang.

It was a snowy day in January, one of those Saturday snows that sneak up on New England drivers because they are a little late and slow with the plowing. Everything was buffered and quiet, the light shining dim and sweet even at midday. The main infusion center was closed, and we were rerouted to the women's cancer infusion ward.

Carmen and Rafe came with me and Peter to celebrate. I had given them each a new costume because they were my chemo superheroes. Rafe was rocking a wizard kit and Carmen's cape was reversible, a queen on one side and a fairy on the other, depending on which powers she needed to summon. They barely took them off for the next four days, hoping the magic would hold.

Kerry was not at Dana Farber that day, and a kind nurse I didn't know efficiently emptied poison into my veins. The snow stopped and sunlight streamed in the windows. Half the chairs were empty, people coming in early, gassing up on their mild infusions, leaving to go grocery shopping or to their grandkid's recital. I chatted with the recent breast cancer survivor in the chair opposite me, full of infectious vim, with wicked cute hair she had decided to keep short.

As I finished, Peter helped me put away teabags, earphones, lavender stress balls, iPad, hankies, meds, snacks, and a cross made of olive wood stained with the oils from my hands with much praying. All of it got chucked into the chemo backpack for the last time.

We stepped out of the elevator to go to the car, and who was standing there before us but my oncologist, Dr. Butrynski, whom we hadn't seen in weeks! We hugged. And fist-bumped. We were all grinning like kids.

We are all by now, because of the pandemic, well-socialized into the social worker catchphrase "The New Normal." It's not comforting when you first hear this phrase after the diagnosis, the death, the breakup, the whatever-it-is that is rocking your universe. But it does give you some sense that competency or healing may come, that your little boat might not always be swamped with grief or anxiety or just too much new information.

On that forty-ninth day of infusion, I finally looked like my worst early imaginings: bald, eyebrowless, slightly wrinkled, occasionally yellow or green or gray-complected instead of rosy. But still myself. A new me. A new normal.

As I closed the door on chemo, I didn't really know what to expect. I'd been warned about the terrible loneliness that comes when treatment ends. I wouldn't be seeing my oncologist every two or three weeks to ask a million questions, to see his kind and confident face, to hear him say, "We'll get you through this," like he often did.

I wouldn't see my sweet savior Nurse Kerry, who had singlehandedly grown millions of white blood cells with her high-speed jokes and gentle knowing of just when to give me an extra warm blanket and shut the door to let me sleep.

Suddenly, all this secure scaffolding—of cards and casseroles, of frequent peeks inside the body and the active war against the cancer by highly trained professionals—it's over. You are into new "Here Be Dragons" unmapped territory where it's just you and your body and its invisible and mysterious workings, moving into a future that may turn out to be an eternity or not very long at all.

I would, of course, have CT scans every three months for the first couple of years, to make sure nothing was regrowing. Then the scans would diminish to twice a year, then once a year until I reached ten years post-treatment.

I was strangely comforted by the fact that Ewing's usually recurs within two years if it is going to do so. I'm pugnacious by nature, and if it was going to fight me, I didn't want to be shadow-boxing some namby-pamby, slow-growing cancer for the next five years. I wanted it to come out soon with its dukes up.

One of the things that messes with your mind big-time when you are liberated from fighting the headwinds of cancer treatment and find yourself suddenly adrift in a becalmed sea of survivorship is the question you carry: what is worthy of your time?

It's cliché to say that getting cancer makes you want to work down a bucket list. It's highly impractical, not to mention expensive, to *only* spend your time after cancer doing things like, say, ziplining through the jungle in Costa Rica.

But before and after the ziplining, there's still laundry. There are bills. The exterminator to call on the dreadful drunken squirrels that have invaded your walls to chew on ancient wiring after eating your fermenting compost (I did NOT survive cancer just to die in a squirrel-induced house fire!). A lot of maintenance and reality gets in the way of Deep and Meaningful Activities After Coming Back from the Dead.

And after treatment, it gets so not just the maintenance, but even everyday joy starts to feel not, well, quite up to snuff for someone who has temporarily avoided being snuffed.

It was a couple of weeks after my last infusion. I had sworn off bills and calls and exercise and exterminators and went back to bed once the kids had gone to school to watch terrible movies and eat chocolate. But it didn't satisfy. It left me feeling like I *should* have been doing yoga on a mountaintop or reading storybooks to Romanian orphans. I got a little depressed, actually.

I wondered: am I ruined for the McPleasures of life because I've had cancer? Am I doomed to forever seek out only high-quality pursuits that improve me in some significant way? Just like some people after cancer submit to rigid, disciplined raw foodist or macrobiotic diets, is the same thing going to happen to me and my leisure time?

In one of the best books I read after treatment, *Dancing in Limbo: Making Sense of Life After Cancer*, two women survivors interviewed fifteen other survivors and distilled their wisdom into canny insights.

One thing they said was, "[Don't be misled to] put the emphasis on 'doing life right' rather than on living. Cancer has forced us to evaluate our lives and understand what is important to us. Once we know what is important, we can begin to do those things that make us feel glad to be alive."

Rumi said this same thing seven or so centuries earlier, only he put it like this:

"Let the beauty you love be what you do."

Jesus, in a great economy of words, maybe would have just said:

"Love."

I decided then that I could kill myself wondering over the next however-many-moments-I-have-left if I was making the most of them. Or I could come to terms with the fact that I would continue to get mad at my kids and my husband and people in traffic. I would be as I always had been: both bad-tempered and shallow and anything but spiritual and beatific sometimes, and sometimes grateful and joy-filled and altruistic. Maybe a little more often than in the Before Times.

But surviving didn't mean I needed to go on a grim-lipped campaign of self-improvement. All I needed to do was notice what makes me glad to feel alive, and do that, because, in the words of Howard Thurman, "what the world needs is people who have come alive."

Chapter 14

HOW TO COME BACK FROM THE DEAD

Two months after chemo ended, when the scorched earth of my scalp was giving way to duckling fuzz, my family and friends threw me a peach fuzz party. We drank bellinis and stood under a constellation of hundreds of get-well cards that an artist friend hung from the tin ceilings of the old parsonage as a sacrament of joy.

My friend Val, a professional storyteller, told resurrection stories from around the world. Stevie took heart-stopping photos. Aisha hung out in the kitchen making on-demand gougères for the throngs of well-wishers that came through: church camp friends, high school and college buddies, parishioners from all of my churches. Rafe turned many of the emails friends had sent me into paper airplanes and hung them from the stairs.

That same day, Carmen turned five and thought the festivities were all for her. She was right. It was for all of us.

A few weeks later, Easter Sunday arrived. My first time back in the pulpit in nearly a year. I probably could have pulled a sermon from DesperatePreacher.com and people would still have been crying, but I preached on "How to Come Back from the Dead," reading John's gospel account of the resurrection.

"In the gospel of John, the Easter story plays like an episode of the old British sitcom *Benny Hill*, with people running on and offscreen in what amounts to hospital johnnies, just missing each other, and the truth.

"Mary Magdalene and Simon Peter and the disciple called 'Beloved' scamper hither and thither, seeing and not seeing and wondering and being afraid while the audience laughs because they are in on the joke. Jesus finally sneaks up behind Mary, who is crying because she can't find his body. "Woman, why are you weeping?" Jesus asks her, even though he already knows the answer.

"Mary looks at him, but doesn't *see* him. She thinks he is the gardener, and she says, "Mister, if you have carried him away, tell me where you have laid him, and I'll take his body off your hands." But Jesus knows a secret. He is not dead, but alive.

"Easter is the holy day of secrets, mysteries, and hidden things. Missing bodies, hidden baskets, eggs that turn up in mid-July when you finally clean behind the couch.

"Two years ago on Easter, I handed out little envelopes with a secret message inside. The envelope read, "Open in case of emergency."

"Last year, on Easter, the secret message was in my heart. Or more literally, in my lung. Three days before Palm Sunday, they found a tumor there. I told a few people about it, but I didn't tell all of you, because I didn't want to make Holy Week about me instead of about God. I didn't realize, then, that it was *all* about God.

"Whatever we go through—the best, and especially the worst, and everything in between—it is *always* about God.

"This Easter, the time for secrets is over. Jesus told Mary Magdalene that she should "go to my siblings and tell them that I am rising, to the One who is your Dad and my Dad, your God and my God." It is too good a secret to keep. God can raise the dead! She was to tell *everybody*. There are no secrets here.

"Maybe some of you might think, because I have survived cancer, I have some secret wisdom. I myself have thought it of other survivors. And maybe we do, simply because we have faced our own deaths, and lived through that particular pain and fear. But that doesn't make me Jesus. It just makes me another Lazarus.

"What you might not know about Lazarus was that he probably didn't live very long after Jesus raised him from the dead. The chief priests planned to put him to death because he was living proof of the supernatural power of Jesus, and they didn't want any competition. Can you imagine? Committing murder to keep people from finding out that the God you are working to get them to believe in is actually alive and well and at work in the world? Talk about sawing off the branch you are sitting on.

"Last year, I stood in this pulpit preaching resurrection, knowing that something inside my body was threatening to kill me. Still, I had trouble believing the danger I was in.

"Mary saw Jesus but didn't recognize him. We can see something so good and be too afraid to really believe in it. The same is true of something really bad. Whether it was stubborn dissociation or wild optimism, I thought that there was no way I had cancer. Wasn't I too alive? Didn't I have too much to do? Didn't I feel too well to possibly be someone who was dying?

"After the pathology report confirmed that it was, in fact, cancer, I remained optimistic. I decided that cancer wasn't going to be all that bad. It would be great experience for ministry! And, if it later killed me, I could always change my mind.

"But my optimism was shaken when I began to look like a sick person, and feel like a sick person. Not because of the cancer, but because of the cure. Some of you know that of all the things that were hard about treatment: mouth sores, nausea, fevers, bone pain, having half a lung removed—probably the hardest thing to endure was losing my hair, being bald, vulnerable, unrecognizable.

"I am a Leo and as such, my hair is my glory. I have occasionally fallen into the idolatrous belief that my hair is who I am.

"When it was my turn, I didn't want to watch all my long red hair go down the drain. I decided to beat chemo to the punch and cut it all off the first week of treatment. Carmen asked for it and put the disembodied ponytail in a blue bowl on top of her dresser. Every once in a while, over the many months of chemo, she would take it out and run her fingers through it. I think she had some idea it was her job to protect it until it could go back on my head after chemo.

"But you know better. You know there's no going back. You heard Rev. Ian preach during Lent about Nicodemus, the Jewish high priest who said sarcastically to Jesus, "Can I go back into my mother's womb and be born again?"

"If there's any secret wisdom I have, it's this. While I called this sermon "How to Come Back from the Dead," the truth is, there's no coming back from the dead. Some things, when they're done, are done. There's no going back to the womb, there's no putting hair back on a chemo patient, and there's no unhearing certain words, words like, "I don't love you anymore and I want a divorce," or words like, "It's cancer," or words like, "There was nothing more we could do."

"The only thing to do when you are facing something deadly, or when something in you dies, is to go on.

"But *how* do you go on? What exactly is one to do? In some ways, it was easy for me to go on from death this past year. They handed me the protocol. I knew that every third Wednesday, Toni Snow or Chelsea Clarke would show up at my front door to take me to chemo infusion. My infusion nurse Kerry would draw some blood, place an IV. The path before me was very clear. I might have been in the darkest forest, but I was on a monorail with a sure conductor. And I knew exactly when it would end: after fourteen cycles of Ifosfamide and Adriamycin.

"But in the meantime, there were those fourteen cycles. Forty-nine days of infusion that felt like they would never end. Arriving back in the same place every two or three weeks didn't feel like forward motion, if pain and nausea and baldness were any indication. There was the early summer day when I lost all my hair, watching it fly away in the breeze. There was the late summer day I let my bald flag fly at the playground for the first time and felt the pity of other moms flooding toward me so much that I wanted to run away.

"There was the early fall day when our family went to Fresh Pond on a walk, and the children covered themselves with milkweed seeds and pretended to be abominable snowmen, and I watched them and cried through my two remaining eyelashes to think that there was a possibility that they might grow up without a mother.

"There was the other early fall day when I felt my first peach fuzz get born, only to feel it fall out again, two weeks later. It would do this eight more times.

"And there were also the many, many days when Carmen would crawl into my lap, and automatically reach her hand up to my slick noggin, and rub it, and say, "You are the most beautiful bald momma in the world." It was manna in the desert. I ate up her words, and just like manna, that food was there the next day, and the next day, and the next. God always provides a way to go on, no matter what wilderness you are in.

"I have always thought of this earthly life as spiritual Tetris. The way behind you is closed. There's no going back there. All you can do is look for the next opening God has provided.

"This spring, the last round of peach fuzz finally bloomed. I couldn't keep my hands off of it. I kept thinking of that ponytail of dead hair, on the top of Carmen's dresser. And I knew what I wanted to do.

"Two weeks ago, our family went back to Fresh Pond, and we brought the ponytail. It was such a strange thing, that hair, so glossy and red and seeming alive, though of course, it wasn't. Some dead things seem to be alive, just like some alive things look like death. We think we know which is which, but often we don't really know.

"I divided the hair into four portions, and we each took one, Peter, the children, and myself. We walked to the milkweed patch, and we waited for a breeze, and we set the hair free.

"It wasn't the mystical moment I imagined, the hair floating into the tree-tops to provide sparrows down to line nests for vulnerable spring nestlings. The hair didn't quite float, rather it *kerplunked* into the field in globby clumps.

"And that's when the strange and holy hilarious thing happened. Two little girls were also there in the field, playing with sticks and violets and laughing in the sunshine.

"They wandered closer and closer to us, until one of them screeched with delight, bent over, and picked up some of my hair. She called her sister over with great excitement, and they began to look everywhere for hair, picking it up where it lay, collecting it into massive fluffy piles.

"I still have no idea what they thought the hair was: Leprechaun yarn? Snuffleupagus fur? It was simply bizarre that they didn't see us right next to them, setting free the hair. Were we in an alternate universe?

"The kids and Peter and I just looked at each other. And then we started laughing and laughing and laughing. The four of us were all in on the secret. None of us had the heart to say anything to the girls. There are some things you can only learn, *should* only learn, when it is time for you to learn them. Knowing hard things is as good as innocence, but there's a time for both innocence and hard knowing. Like with Mary Magdalene, there is a time for mere looking, and a time for seeing.

"Some of you are on the other side of innocence, and have seen too much. You are also Lazaruses. You have survived cancer, or heartbreak, or abuse, or terrible grief. For some of you, the 'chemo,' the great harrowing thing that healed you, didn't last fourteen cycles but lasted fourteen years.

"But knowing there is no coming back from the dead, you went on. You fell in love again. Or you made peace with the idea of your physical death. Or you found God, or found us, which sometimes amounts to the same thing.

"Some of you have yet to encounter death in a big way. When it comes for you, in the form of the death of someone you love, or the death of your dreams, or illness or depression, know this: you can go kicking or screaming, or you can be *ready*. If you start practicing going on with the little deadlies right now, when big deadlies come along, it'll be second nature.

"How do you do this? How do you go on when there is not a chemo protocol laid out for you? Last week, the choir sang these words:

I feel like going on…I feel like going on…though trials mount, at every hand, I feel like going on.

"Here are some ways Jesus has given us to go on:

Pray. As you can, not as you can't. Don't wait until you can pray with noble intention. Pray with tears and snot running down your face for what you really want.

Tell a friend what you are going through, or like I did, tell five hundred.

Look for beauty. Start with the mirror.

Be vulnerable and naked though it terrifies you. Let your bald flag fly, and see what happens.

Let people feed you.

Spend time with children who love you. If you think there are no children who love you, we have children at the church, all around you, loving children. Believe them when they call you beautiful.

Writing is catharsis. Write it all out. Treat your feelings like beloved houseguests, but not permanent housemates.

Keep coming to church, even if it's hard. We'll be good to you here.

Spend time in nature, God's raw ingredients and the first things She called Good.

Take lots of showers and baths: these are baptisms for every day.

Sing songs in your car at the top of your lungs: Bach, or Beyoncé. God made both of them.

Count your blessings. And like the poet Marge Piercy said, whatever you can't bless, get ready to make new.

"This year's gift for each of you is from Fresh Pond, a milkweed seed. Take the seed and set it free on the wind. The seed knows how to go on. And so do you.

After church that Sunday, we rode to the family feast at my cousin's house in the burbs. Rafe piped up from the back seat, "You know, Mom, your sermon was very emotional. Like, half the people in church were weeping. And you know who was weeping the most? *Dad.* There were tears streaming down his face." Peter vehemently denied it.

It's been ten years since I preached that sermon. I have accumulated many more possible deaths, and each one has made me a little more unusually alive, and even more grateful than I would have thought possible.

That spring, the kids and I went to Les and Sam's house in the woods, and I built a fire and burned the box of journals I kept from age thirteen to age twenty-five—journals I long fantasized about being the first thing to save in a house fire. Now I was hand-feeding them into the flames.

I wasn't killing my old selves. Wounds and joy were subsumed back into my being. I finally realized that I carried all the old Mollys within me, and didn't need to preserve them in amber.

That summer, determined not to be a scaredy-cat anymore, I decided to make good on a longtime dream to swim the length of historic Walden Pond. Walden is a kettle pond, formed by glaciers, and impossibly deep in the middle, the thickest of thin places.

I had long wondered what lurked there, in those depths? Leviathan, Loch Ness, a herd of snapping turtles? Would I survive cancer just to get a cramp and drown in the middle of a pond in suburban Massachusetts?

I knew I had the skill. But did I have the courage? A mom friend from Rafe's school came with me. Alison and I brought her daughter's Hannah Montana boogie board and took turns strapping it to our feet as we inched our way across the pond, radiant with victory at the end of our odyssey. After that, I swam it on my own, many times, every swim a baptism.

Three years after chemo ended, as I felt less and less like a cancer patient in recovery and more and more like a whole person, I knew other resurrection stories needed telling, particularly, that of my sweet, scrappy church in Somerville. I wrote down everything we had done to come back from the dead. Pilgrim Press turned it into a beautiful little book, *Real Good Church*, which for at least one or two days cracked the #16,000 mark on Amazon.

When people read the book and wanted me to come teach them at their churches and denominational gatherings, at first, I said, "I don't do that," my fear of public speaking eclipsing even the fear of death.

"But—you're a preacher!" they would say in protest.

"That's different," I'd respond. "They're like my family."

God interrupted, and Peter did too. He said, "Go. Say yes to everyone who asks. This won't last, and you'll learn a lot."

He was right: I have learned a lot. He was wrong: it has lasted. I still get to travel all over the country meeting dear and wise people of faith, all of whom have made my life bigger.

Then the most terrifying and exciting public speaking request came (that is, until Oprah invites me on *Super Soul Sunday*. Any day now): my denomination asked me to be the opening preacher at our biennial national gathering, with thousands of my peers.

It was a victory for my whole sweet church. For years, we had labored and prayed and painted and worried and organized and gave until it hurt and kept giving until it started to feel good. We did All The Things necessary to become a viable and vital faith community that would outlive and outlast any single person leaving, me included.

After accepting the invitation to preach, I did the most important first thing: bought the boots and the statement necklace.

I spent the next ten months writing that sermon, and when the time came, my people drove all night and got on planes to the Midwest even though they were afraid of flying. They showed up, my little church that contained multitudes. Carmen and Rafe and bestie Sue and my godkids and our drag-queen-in-residence Serenity Jones and about thirty other Firsties from the diaspora were there.

The afternoon before opening worship, we saw the news that the Supreme Court had made marriage equality the law of the land. Megan, our student minister, and their girlfriend ran out and got matching tattoos to commemorate it. You have never seen joy like thousands of lefty Christians in a convention center in Cleveland celebrating the end of a heresy and the honoring of love.

That night on a big fancy stage before thousands of adorable church folks, I preached, shaking a little in my boots, and then the whole Somerville crew rushed the stage and we ended with a dance flash mob to Sara Bareilles's "Brave."

Of course we did. Our church had become a place where the kids, now numbering in the dozens, had started running down to the front of the sanctuary *every* week at the end of worship expecting to boogie. Because nothing says resurrection like a dance party.

I did get on that stage with one more secret, however. I hadn't told all those beautiful souls who jumped up to boogie that night that I had gotten a call. Not a phone call. A God-call. It started as an email I read walking to a predawn exercise class on a frigid winter day. It was from the search committee of First Congregational Church of Berkeley, California—did I want to apply to become their next senior minister?

For twelve years, Peter and I had had a five-year plan to move to the Bay Area: toward family we missed, toward sun and mountains, and because it was the only other place tolerably progressive enough for us. It was a hard decision. I had a 99 percent approval rating in Somerville. We'd finally punched through the plateau into real growth, more equilibrium, and little conflict. We'd just bought our first home, on the same block as bestie Sue and Jason, where Rafe and Carmen would play hide-and-seek with their kids, Ruby and Abe, until well after dark. I did a DIY kitchen reno and had a whole drawer for Tupperware. For once, everything fit.

Was I willing to blow up a perfectly beautiful life, and risk turning my more or less completely content kids against me forever, for a call?

Yes. Because, as my spiritual director used to say, if you're done growing, you might as well die. Anything else is biding time in a satin-lined coffin. In my heart of hearts, I knew that I needed a new challenge, and so did the church.

When we got home from Synod, we told the children. They fell to the floor, sobbing and fetal. After a few minutes of gentle weeping, they raised their heads to ask in unison, "Can we get a pool?" No, we answered gently. More weeping, and again the raising of heads, this time asking, "Can we get a hot tub?" Yes, most likely.

I said goodbye to First Church Somerville, to Dibbie and Marlin and Ian and Melissa and Jenny, and 350 other people who had seen me through the valley of the shadow of death and helped me live again. At one of many going-away dinners, I told them my twelve years with them had been the happiest in my life. We all get a few really tremendous loves in our lives, if we are lucky. Love is a vocation, love is a verb, love is a muscle—and the more we use it, the stronger it gets. But some loves defy these metaphors of agency and effort. They are not "work" at all. Somerville was such a love.

Our farewell came in January, six months after we flash-mobbed to "Brave" on that stage in Cleveland, at a winter prom in the church basement. Peter and I endured roasting and spot-on skits and the giving of many gifts and the wearing of actual prom queen and king sashes. And of course, we danced, bravely.

I got on a plane, all by myself, and flew west. The kids and Peter stayed behind to finish the school year.

I entered a short chapter of living solo, settling into a tiny house in Berkeley. I would learn to navigate a new city. I would learn how to pastor and fall in love with a new people. I would keep dancing—this time, through fire.

Chapter 15

CHURCH ON FIRE

Everything that is still alive is still growing. The fact of its aliveness—*your* aliveness—also means it can be cut down, burned down, killed. This is what makes life so tender, and so terrible.

In many ways, our move to California was right on time. I was five years cancer-free (in other words: it was a good bet I wasn't going to die before my new church recouped their investment). The kids were going into fifth and ninth grade, liminal times when we thought they'd be open to a new adventure.

I wanted to be closer to my sisters Tessa and Sam, to bestie Sarah and to Peter's dear family, having adventures with them during crucial years while the kids were still with us and before lumbago set in.

My new church in Berkeley was bigger and wealthier than Somerville, and it felt like an interesting challenge: a mix of my suburban Boston church's stability and Somerville's wonderful strangeness. Northern California, with its aching majesty and warm-coolness, had always called to me. Everything was coming up rosemary.

I should have known better.

I often offer this shorthand to people in distress: "everything turns out all right in the end. If it's not all right, it's not the end." And then nuance it: If it *is* all right, don't get too attached, framing the moment and hanging it above your sofa.

Because life has a habit of cycling through unpredictable sine waves of equilibrium and disequilibrium. Bad things happen, then thorny problems resolve, and if you are lucky, you live long enough for life to get hard again.

On my first night in the Berkeley tiny house I was renting until Peter and the kids arrived, I realized how alone I was for the first time in a very long time. I craved aloneness, and was also terrified by it.

I took care to hang up the six outfits I brought that said "quirky, creative professional," clothes I imagined a progressive Christian senior minister of a storied anchor church would wear.

I made myself a dinner of eggs laid by the hens who shared the backyard, fried in real butter, which had been banned from our dairy-free house for years. I had a good poop in the compost toilet and hoped my effortlessly cool surfer-schoolteacher host wasn't in the garden accidentally overhearing. I showered in the outdoor shower sheltered by redwoods. The constellations above me had shifted with my new latitude. Dr. Bronner's bubbles lifted off into the night.

To be a longtime mother and/or wife alone on her own is a strange and wonderful thing. It's a sudden downshift in gears. Muscles that have been pumping so hard for years suddenly meet no resistance when it is only one's own bodily and emotional needs to consider, and you find yourself flying downhill, your hair streaming behind you in the breeze.

Then it was bedtime the shadow side of aloneness arrived with it. I spent a half-hour clearing daddy longlegs from the loft bed. I drank a glass of wine or three and watched entirely too much *Call the Midwife*, willing myself into sleepiness.

I woke up the next day and walked up the street toward the Berkeley hills and First Congregational Church. Over the next weeks, I cultivated the buds of four hundred new relationships in my church. I studied the systems, strategies, and sacred cows of our community, listening for both history and future. I leaned into panic attacks driving across the Bay Area's many bridges after reading entirely too much about the overdue fault lines that webbed my new home.

During my interview process, at an all-church Q&A, someone had asked me, "How will you bring stability to our church?" Without thinking, I blurted out, "I don't bring stability. I bring instability!" Raucous laughter erupted from some corners, side-eye from others. I tried to save my answer somehow by explaining, "If it weren't for the occasional disequilibrium breaking into our lives, our systems and structures would never change. Then where would expansion, inclusion, a growth mindset come from?"

But my church already knew disequilibrium. They had suffered three fires decades earlier, and some church members had watched homes burn to the ground by wildfire. One of the first sermons I preached was to remind them of how fire had made way for new growth: the 1967 fire, arriving in the middle of the civil rights movement and the free speech movement's ground zero at UC Berkeley across the street, had raised more in capital campaign funds than the church needed for rebuilding. They turned the surplus into startup capital for neighboring African American entrepreneurs and program funds to foster dialogue across difference at the university.

Those early days were heady, long, rewarding, and curious. I noticed that the core congregation was a bit grayer than I had expected, and the pews a bit emptier (I checked my breath. Not it.). The long-standing church treasurer warned me of an impending financial impasse: we couldn't sustain our current staffing levels, but a female pastor firing staff her first year wasn't a good look. Next, a group of twelve lovely, anxious people made an appointment with me to offer a short history of recent church conflicts—and get my vote on them.

In the meantime, my family back home was suffering without me. While I binged Netflix every night after a pell-mell day of meetings and emails, Peter was workaholicking through his last three months as an IT director at Harvard. Rafe was beginning to get into trouble in the unsupervised afternoons and battling with Peter almost every night, with Carmen caught in the emotional crossfire.

By the time we were all reunited and in our new home in early August, met by a welcome basket full of goodies from a cherished parishioner, I naively hoped we'd met our new beginning. By September, all hell broke loose.

Rafe quickly found that no one he met wanted to come to our remote neighborhood to hang out. Instead of a whirlwind metropolis, we were in an island community where high-school kids still clung to their best friends from kindergarten. Loneliness supercharged by ADD gutted his self-esteem, leading to isolation and defensiveness, which made him even lonelier and more depressed in a vicious cycle.

Even sunny-souled Carmen had trouble making friends. Facing the mean girl mafia of fifth grade, she lost her mojo. She took to sitting alone at recess. One day, she was reading at the edge of the playground and got concussed by a wayward basketball to the face. That was the last straw. Carmen has always had Big Feelings, but for the first time in her life, she'd tipped over into something beyond my pay grade. She lost her appetite. She stopped reading books and making art. Gone were the impromptu skits featuring characters such as Bobitino the French-Italian Waiter, Zach the Bruh Chef, and Mintsel Handsome the Faded Vaudeville Actor. Her tears were bottomless, dark, and terrifying.

One night, I held my tiny ten-year-old as she wept and admitted, "I don't want to kill myself, but I do think a lot about what it would be like to go to sleep and not wake up in the morning. And then I feel guilty because I don't want to leave you and Dad—I know it would hurt you too much." My tween-age daughter was admitting to me her own Random Tuesday death wish.

The next morning after drying her eyes and packing her off to school, I showed up to my office hours at a local café and promptly burst into sobs in front of the two parishioners coming to me that day for pastoral care. Both mothers themselves, they mothered me.

Meanwhile, my sister Tessa in Kauai was struggling with poor mental health. After years of experiencing spousal abuse, her marriage ended. She lost custody of her children to her ex in the divorce, a wounding blow. One night, she took too many pills and fell asleep on top of a cliff, hoping to die. She woke up alone the next day, but felt this was only a brief reprieve from her inevitable early death.

I flew there to take her surfing and feed her and pray with her and try to help her become curious about the rest of her life and what might happen next. On the last day of our visit, when I dropped her off at the lettuce farm where she was currently working for a safe place to lay her head, I kissed her, rolled up the window of the rental sedan, and drove down the red dirt road, not knowing if I would ever see her face again.

Two weeks later, I got in the car after meeting with a tattoo artist in San Francisco to finally plan my scar-enhancing Holy Spirit ink. My phone buzzed: a short series of texts from the church's business manager.

"There's a little chimney fire in Pilgrim Hall, I'm sure we can manage."

"So, the fire has spread to the roof. Firefighters are here and everybody is out safe."

"Fire has spread to the sanctuary. It's an official conflagration."

I said I'd be right there and drove across the Bay Bridge to Berkeley, clutching the wheel as I watched an enormous column of smoke rising into the ether from what could only be our church.

Dozens had gathered. All three local network news affiliates buzzed around, as did a number of independent insurance adjusters vying for our business.

Then there were my people, drawn by the breaking news alert and by a wildfire of texts and phone calls, watching their church home burn. The large assembly that had held their wedding receptions and anniversary parties, the nooks where they had played hide-and-seek as children, the nursery where they had first entrusted their precious bundle to another human being, all erased by the inferno. Some were crying. Some were solemn. Some sought to comfort me, aware of how much work this loss would mean.

"We've been through this before," said Bonnie. "Our church is the people and not the building," said Becky. "Thank goodness no one was hurt. The rest is just stuff." Moe and Dan got calmly to work, talking to the fire chief, making the right phone calls, keeping the ambulance chasers at bay.

The staff and I found each other and reconnoitered in the parking lot of the senior center across the street. We could have cried, and did a little, but mostly decided to laugh instead. "If I'd known this was going to happen, I wouldn't have cleaned my office!" our music director Derek said. "We just got that new bathroom!" Rev. Kit lamented. "I only used it twice!"

Four hours later, when the fire was finally out, I stood in our gorgeous, ruined church, gobs of ceiling spackling pews, the drip, drip from heat-twisted steel struts gently raining onto the floor. I prayed that the congregation wouldn't remember the sermon I preached six months earlier about how God longs to set the church on fire. Metaphorically.

I said then that God sparks controlled burns to pare away that which does not serve Her purposes, to free up space and energy for new directions. We were about to find out if that was true.

As a coda to our misery, grief, and exhaustion, thirty-eight days later, Donald J. Trump was elected president of the United States. Suffice to say that the Bay Area, and my congregation in particular, took it *very* personally. We had planned an Election Night watch party event with BYOB, pantsuits, and MSNBC. Dueling dance playlists (depending on who won) were cued up for the end of the evening. We clinked glasses, all but certain that we would be toasting the first woman president before the night was out and rocking out to Beyoncé's "Run the World (Girls)." Who knew, as the pinot flowed, that we'd soon be crooning along to Gloria Gaynor's "I Will Survive."

When they called Florida, some left to grieve privately. Some cried openly. Most of us sat stunned. And when there were only about twenty of us left, we did the only thing we knew how to do in that moment: we turned off the TV, turned up the music, and made slow, sweeping circles around each other, leaping, spinning, falling to the ground, rising up again.

People of fire know how to rebuild. More than once, the people in my church had found beauty from ashes, garnered a new vision, and set themselves to make it reality. Truth be told, I was a little excited about the work before us. I had been getting nervous that our church was a little *too* together, and what good could I, the disruptor, the bringer of zany, impossible ideas, be to them? If it ain't broke, you don't fix it.

The Blue Sky team, so named for our roofless ruin out of which you could see daylight, formed to imagine how our disaster could turn out to be a blessing for others. We were stewards of an amazing piece of real estate: could we incorporate affordable housing into our rebuild? We had built a senior housing development thirty years earlier. We could do it again.

The Bay Area was at that moment, and still is, embroiled in a devastating, immoral, unaffordable housing and homelessness crisis. Boomers in the Hills, middle-class professionals who had bought their homes in the early seventies, were now millionaires on paper while down in the Flats, more people were living and dying in squalor on the street every year. Across the street from Lululemon's $80 leggings, under the bridge to the Berkeley Marina, hundreds of human beings lived beside mountains of decaying detritus. What could one single church do to help? But some of us wanted to try anyhow.

So began a conversation that continued for nearly four years, and lit a dozen more metaphorical fires at church. Almost immediately, people took sides. Some worried that if we tore up our parking lot to make room for housing, we would displace current members. Others, eager to do something to respond to the human misery around us, were agog that their fellow church-mates could compare their need for a parking spot to a neighbor's need for four walls and a roof. Some stayed out of the fray entirely; others wanted to postpone the conversation until things cooled down because church conflict was threatening to burn down what was left of our church.

A year went by, and we were no closer to a consensus. Just like the nation, we were becoming more and more polarized in our perspectives. We had scheduled a meeting to talk about the dream of affordable housing for the first Sunday in December—or to table it for a future (read: never) date.

The Monday before the scheduled big meeting, I was in New Orleans with a group of dear friends, the daily devotional writers for our denomination, for our semi-annual meeting. We were having cocktails and bantering at the end of a long day of writing when my lap buzzed. My sister Emily back in

New Hampshire sent me a link to an article from the Philippines, where our brother Jesse had been living:

> AN AMERICAN national was found dead Tuesday dawn, December 5, hanging inside a restroom in the detention cell of the National Bureau of Investigation (NBI)-Central Visayas in Cebu City.
>
> Jesse Golden Phinney, 42, who hailed from Massachusetts, USA, allegedly tied a belt around his neck at 1 a.m. inside the NBI 7 detention cell's comfort room.
>
> "He was supposed to be facing inquest proceedings in court for human trafficking and violations of the Anti-Child Abuse Law. When we interviewed him, he was fine," Atty. Patricio Bernales Jr., regional director of the NBI 7, said.

Was this some kind of *Weekly World News* situation? Perhaps an elaborate prank that our jokey gadabout brother was playing on us? My mind looked for a painless answer. At the same moment, my body drove me outside, stabbing at the phone ineffectually as I tried to call my family. I sobbed on the phone to my dad, and then my sister Emily, who confirmed that it was true: Jesse was dead. "Oh, Jesse, what have you done?" I said over and over.

My friends bundled me into a cab and took me back to the hotel, where Quinn, Kaji, and Donna rubbed my feet, listened to me ramble, brought me wine and tea, and held me while the tears cascaded. As I ruminated and perseverated and then apologized, Donna stopped me short and said, "There's nothing you can do right now that is wrong."

Kaji had her assistant rebook my flight for early in the morning, heading home to Boston now, and they tucked me in bed, to face whatever came next.

The flight to Boston was one of the more terrifying moments of my life. Storm winds rocked us in every direction and threw us north at warp speeds. My seatmate, a Black documentary filmmaker named Llewellyn, held my hand, bought me a vodka tonic, and listened while I poured out the whole sordid story for him. How we had just seen Jesse very much alive two weeks earlier when he flew to California from Cebu on a lark for Thanksgiving, bearing gifts and bad uncle jokes. I didn't know what to believe because I knew my brother to be many things: adventurous, charming, mysterious, restless—and one thing I knew for certain is that he loved life too much to ever take his own.

I spent the next three days with my father, stepmother, and sister Emily, contacting the State Department and the press, arranging to have his body brought home for an independent autopsy, doing whatever we could to get to the truth about Jesse. It was a quest that would consume me, as I enlisted a PI with a thick Boston accent who chased leads and tried to unravel a story that became more knotted as he went.

A respected pathologist informed us he had been beaten before he died and that the marks on his neck were not consistent with a suicidal hanging. We were vindicated. But to what end? We would never get to the whole truth from seven thousand miles away, in a country known for its extrajudicial killings and vigilante justice.

In the meantime, I still had a day job. The big meeting to determine whether or not we moved forward with low-income housing on our campus was still on for that Sunday. I wanted to be there. I believed so much in my own powers of persuasion, so wholly that my cause was God's cause, that I knew I *had* to be there.

About seventy people crowded into our smallish chapel. And then, as often happens in churches when anxiety is high, some of the most anxious people found relief in scapegoating the pastor. One person suggested that

I must not really care about old people if I was willing to sacrifice parking spots. Whether they agreed with him or not, nobody challenged that idea.

Perhaps emboldened by that warning shot, another man, Arthur, slowly got to his feet and took direct aim at me. As though he had rehearsed it, he said, "I've lost faith in our church's leadership, and I have decided to pull my pledge immediately. I invite anybody else to join me in stopping your giving as a sign of protest."

He was diverting a significant sum of money away from our church because we were having a conversation. He smiled as he spoke, and then sat down.

Silence permeated the room. I waited for someone, anyone to defend me, to talk about their support for my leadership. Or even better, to say, "This is a conversation we are having as a whole church about where God might be calling us. It is not a referendum on Molly. Let's stay focused on the main issue."

But the silence stood, and I took it very hard. I was furious and crushed. I had moved across the country for them, uprooting my children who still hadn't forgiven me and who were still struggling emotionally. I had worked long hours for them, before and since the fire, trying to turn this ship toward the future in a sea of declining membership and metro Californian indifference to liberal Christianity.

Most of all, I was raw with grief, confusion, and rage that my brother had been murdered only six days before, in a distant country, unreachable, unknowable. In that silence, eons passed, enough for me to cycle through a thousand picket signs on my peevish personal protest. One read, *I didn't survive cancer and then move all the way across the country for this shit!* The other, *I didn't live to mother my children so I could spend my life force fighting about parking!*

Before the silence became unbearable, someone changed the subject and the conversation went on. After the meeting, I had hard words for my closest ally because he hadn't publicly championed me, then immediately regretted turning on him, and proceeded to ugly-cry the whole drive home.

The following Sunday, as I stood at the back of the sanctuary getting ready to lead worship, I found myself shaking and barely able to hold back tears. Gripped by panic at the thought of having to act natural and nice in front of this group of people I thought had cared about me, but who had watched me get crucified without saying a word, I didn't know what to do.

I grabbed Carmelle, a no-nonsense and deeply faithful elder, on her way in to worship. "I can't face them after what happened last week. How do I do this?" She unflinchingly looked me in the eyes, and said, "God is in there somewhere, in every one of them. Sometimes, you have to look a little harder to see it."

Years later, I have more perspective on how that debacle unfolded. Both the church leadership and I have worked closely with the Lombard Mennonite Peace Center and its director emeritus, Richard Blackburn, to understand how to embody a non-anxious presence, how to be self-differentiated when herd mentality takes over, and how to separate current emotional content from old conflicts operating incognito.

Many of us have learned how to challenge destructive behaviors so that we don't have all-church meetings that devolve into personal attacks or festivals of scapegoating. And we've learned to anticipate some degree of conflict around transitions and anxious times, when herd instinct comes into play.

But in that moment with Carmelle, I learned that you can blame the blamers back, or take responsibility for your own reactivity and functioning. As Richard Blackburn says, "Christ exposes the false nature of the scapegoating mechanism. We no longer have to follow the crowd."

The breakthrough finally came during my last session of the Clergy Clinic and Family Emotional Process training at the Peace Center this past year. We were asked to review a time when we had not functioned at our best in a church conflict, and God gave me a new insight about that wrenching December meeting. It was easy to make Arthur the villain of the story. He was older, white, male, moneyed, and behaved very badly.

But he was only playing one part in the drama. I had a role too. What the hell was I doing in a meeting like that, six days after my brother's death? Why didn't I take that Sunday off and leave it to other leaders to carry this dream forward? If God's dreams for us really weren't about my preferences, if it was *really* about God's hopes for the whole church, I could have trusted the whole church to take the conversation forward, even if it was somewhere I didn't want it to go, while I tended the wounds of my family.

The truth was: I thought of my doggedness, my heart for the poor, and my ability to often inspire people to bold action as clear-cut virtues. I thought if I could just work harder and charm more forcefully, it would all come right.

But as Flannery O'Connor once said, "even our virtues will be burned away" as we get ready to enter heaven. I thought getting cancer had helped me shed workaholism forever and had given me a new spirit of *carpe diem*. I thought I was done being the good girl and a pleaser, but those "virtues" had crept back in sneaky new disguises.

I felt like a failure and spent many nights crying and wondering if God had made a terrible mistake in sending me to Berkeley. Hadn't it all gone wrong since we arrived? Does even God sometimes set a controlled burn in the wild woods, but then, horrified, watch as it takes out the adjacent village?

Often in church and other unruly human settings, people lead and speak from their wounds. As you can imagine, this doesn't go very well. The hardest part is, they don't even realize they are wounded. People can become so dissociated from their own pain that they are like the Black Knight from *Monty Python and the Holy Grail* who has had three limbs lopped off and still insists "it's only a flesh wound!"

These people often succeed in displacing pain from their personal and familial situations onto safer others who are close, but not too close. Pastors, who are often both the most responsible *and* the most vulnerable people in the family system of a church, make a great target. Richard Blackburn is fond of quoting an Episcopal priest who once noted "the clergy collar is the screen upon which parishioners project their home movies."

Arthur's hurts didn't excuse his treatment of me, or how he weaponized his personal disappointment. But in doing my own work, I came to understand how much unmetabolized grief was at work, not just in Arthur but through the entire congregation. Grief not only from the fire but also from all the fires that were burning down the world as they knew it in an age of disruption and relentless change. In retrospect, my movement to action—pushing for a housing project, pushing for answers about my brother's death—was a way of bypassing my own grief at all that had gone wrong, rather than sit painfully with the ambiguity and the mess of life.

Three of our church leaders, Leonard, Julie, and Sara were calm captains of the ship through this time. Sara said to me, "The challenge is to be patient with pain, our own and other people's Especially when we say what we want—our highest values—but we still have to process what living into those values will cost us."

Our grief and anxiety did not succeed in stopping our mission. The conversation was put on hiatus for nearly two years. In the meantime, we had a series of tender but liberating community conversations about all kinds of things that *weren't* affordable housing. Those circles became opportunities to identify the gremlins of old grief that had nothing to do with the matter at hand, to learn how to respond to destructive behaviors by becoming more capable upstanders, and to practice disagreeing while still loving one another.

When it came time to talk about affordable housing again, we were much closer to a design for our new community center that would replace the burned husk of our building. Realizing that our insurance company had shortchanged us by millions of dollars, we had a financial crisis looming—and an opportunity. Leasing part of our parking lot to a low-income housing developer would gift us several million dollars, money we could invest in our church's future.

This time, the call to build housing came not from the Blue Sky idealists but from our pragmatic treasurer and other longtime members. The obvious benefit to our church made it a safer and more concrete topic, and let previously polarized people re-engage from new, more moderated positions.

When we finally took the vote, yoking the new community center design to the decision to put up housing on the other end of our campus, 93 percent of the congregation said yes. We could do well by doing good, and we got there together in God's timing, with a lot of collateral growth and healing.

My friend Rev. Lynice Pinkard talks about authentic community—and the "stubborn loyalty" that marks it and makes it. "We recognize that community is a naturally therapeutic context that fosters maturation, healing, and growth for its members. Stubbornly loyal participants band together to provide stabilizing connections and correctives, and to offer support when personalities fragment or boundaries break down," she says. "Community is available to help bind up what is broken. This 'stubborn support and confrontation for growth' is our spirituality.

"We (also) recognize that community is a place where both good friends and predictable frustrators are present, needed, valued, respected, incorporated, and indeed learned from in genuine dialogue. Stubbornly inclusive participants do not give up on the irritating or withdraw into the conforming, but rather welcome the tensions of both."

For Lynice, these are not just words. She literally worked herself out of a job at our sister church in Oakland. It is now led entirely by volunteers and run by people of color together with white folks, neurodivergent and neurotypical, poor and financially secure folks, housed and unhoused, all ages, and all mental and physical abilities. It is not easy to lead like this. It is not a megachurch, nor in danger of becoming one. But they do incredibly brave, world-changing work because they have become, in a phrase Lynice herself coined, "feral Christians" with little to lose.

Lynice goes on, "Community is a collision of egos, a furnace for welding steel-hard opinions, a crucible for melting the hard ores of self-interests into common Love goals. It offers the pain of not getting our own way, (and) the promise of finding a third way altogether."

As much as I sometimes hate that this is how durable, real community gets built—through this collision of egos and melting of self-interest—I recognize from going through conflict again and again that it really is the only way.

Rafe started struggling in earnest after Jesse's death, as our church conflict was reaching its apex.

He was barely going to school. He slept all day and was awake a lot of the night. Days would go by without him showering or brushing his teeth. He discovered the wonders of weed and its capacity to wrap all that is uncomfortable or unwelcome in a soft haze. We didn't know any of his new friends or their parents since the move, so had no way to do the back-channeling that parents of teens do to try to figure out if their kid is all right or if they are in real danger.

Rafe lionized my brother Jesse, taking his death very hard, and was also angry at him for the anguish he had caused. It didn't help that people kept saying the sprouting Rafe was looking more and more like Jesse. Jesse's widow gifted him hand-me-downs. Rafe put a homemade tattoo of Jesse's initials on his ankle. His sweet and jokey demeanor would suddenly give way to fits of rage if we challenged him too much, or if something didn't go his way. He tried different ADD meds, some of them with terrible psychological effects: panic attacks, dissociation. Peter became more authoritarian; I became more permissive. We were undermining and second-guessing each other, and stressing our marriage to a breaking point.

Finally, we decided to all go to therapy together. We talked about what limits we might set and what it meant to follow through—were we willing to kick him out if things escalated? Call the cops if he put a fist through the wall again? Pay for therapeutic boarding school, or Outward Bound? Stop drinking our dinnertime wine to set an expectation for sobriety? Stop working and take medical leave to focus on parenting him more presently?

Our family egos were getting forged on the anvil of stored-up grief, trauma, loneliness, dislocation, depression, and anxiety, substance use and abuse, workaholism, and teenage hormones. It was slow work, both very painful and transformational.

There were wrecking-ball moments along the way when I worried that he would end up on hard drugs, dead by twenty. After one therapy session, I sobbed in the car to Peter, "I just keep seeing him, in my mind's eye, living in the homeless encampment near the freeway underpass, spare changing. Our little boy!" Peter answered, "Our job right now is neither to catastrophize nor be in denial, but just to stay in this moment, to set limits, and love him."

Peter and I kept going to the therapist long after Rafe stopped, for parenting advice and action plans. Again and again, we heard, "Using substances isn't something he is doing *to you*. It is just something he is doing, period—to try to feel better, or at least feel less."

We found a school that was part therapeutic boarding school and part wilderness camp in Colorado that was affordable if we plundered his college fund. We decided it was better to invest in him now. And frankly, he wanted to get away from us as much as we needed the break.

He went off to Colorado and learned how to rock climb, backpack, and mountain bike. He found his first girlfriend. Some of his arguments came to blows in the rough and tumble culture there, and he continued to experiment with substances. He also found confidence in math tutoring and discovered that some of the kids there were "far more fucked up than me," which put his own hurts and gifts into perspective. Metal must be fired to find its strength. And mettle must be tested to discover its worth.

At the end of that year, he decided he was ready to be home for senior year, and he entered the alternative high school in town, where he ended up graduating six months early, thanks to the amazing teachers and administrators who knew just how to gamify success and cheer him over the finish line.

He has spent the last couple of years working blue-collar jobs and working to understand himself, through books, mentors, therapy, and transcending ego through the occasional use of psilocybin. In a recent heart-to-heart, he told me, "You have to understand, in those bottoming-out years, I was exhausted from everything: the years of ruthless bullying, the move, my own ADD brain, and having to start over again and again. I had a good childhood, but not an easy one. For a long time, I was in a quantum state of being terrified of everyone and everything. That made me take an adversarial stance in every new room I walked into. But I know more of who I am now, and don't need to prove myself to anyone except the people I'm closest to."

For a long time, Rafe could not admit how scared and defended he was. The relentless exasperation he felt from the adults in his life had made him less and less motivated to even halfheartedly try to be the kid he thought we wanted. He felt constantly judged and dismissed by the people who were supposed to love him unconditionally. We withheld approval, hoping he'd change, which felt to him like we were withholding our love. He in turn refused to comply until we accepted him as he was.

Our turning point, though I didn't know it then, was a family therapy session in which Peter and I admitted that the root of our anger and disappointment was full-on fear. We were deeply worried about him, scared for his safety and future, and insecure in our parenting. Seeing our vulnerability allowed him to take off his own armor. He later told me, "When you admitted in therapy, 'We're having a hard time, and we need your help,' that changed everything."

Parents are their children's first gods. We learned from Rafe that like a good God, we needed to be magnets, not puppet masters. Vulnerable gods, not strong-man gods. *Tzimtzum* gods who can leave room for their children's freedom and screwing up, and who always leave the light on so they can find their way home.

If there's anything I've learned about fire after five years of living with Northern California wildfires, it's this: if it's a good winter with lots of rain, that just means more fuel is going to grow for the following summer's fires. Blessings of growth give way to burning, in an endless cycle. But we can learn from the previous fires things we need to be ready for the next one.

Two weeks after Heather Heyer was killed in the streets of Charlottesville after the infamous Unite the Right rally, the white supremacist cult the Proud Boys came to town to try to make Berkeley a new seedbed for the far-right. It was their MO to make inroads in liberal cities like Berkeley. If they could catch fire there, it would make an outsized statement about their viability and power.

Our church invited other faith communities to gather in our sanctuary. Six hundred people showed up to pray and sing and chant against the powers of evil, this tornado touching down in our own town. Some of us stayed on at the sanctuary to set up soup and guard personal belongings while the rest of us marched downtown to sing down the white supremacists. The day ended without casualties when thousands of counterprotesters, church ladies arm in arm with Antifa, showed up to stand our ground against several dozen of them. The Proud Boys have not returned since. We ended the day back at church, eating homemade soup and good chocolate.

The pandemic brought our congregation together in other unprecedented ways as we laugh and weep together in Zoom coffee hour, which oddly makes for much deeper sharing than in-person does. We have had the most conflict-free season since my arrival. We are currently shopping RFPs to low-income housing developers and have finally submitted new building design plans to the City of Berkeley to replace our burned-out building.

We are accompanying a Honduran refugee family, two sisters and their four children. They are a study in survivorship and put our lives in perspective every day. The youngest, Santos, was a surprise baby. Maria, his mother, was roofied and raped at a family party and didn't even realize she was pregnant until she gave birth to him nine months later.

This past December, we filmed a Christmas Eve special for virtual church. Maria was cast as Mary, another surprise mother of a miracle baby, and Santos as Jesus. Together they cuddled in the husk of our burned building as the sun set overhead. She laid him gently in the crèche and lit a single candle, which she passed offscreen to us. She is still reminding us how to look for the stars when the roof is gone.

Sister Tessa is living in a shelter on Kauai, but alive. Carmen found a bestie, who later moved three thousand miles away, and decided that her most reliable local best friends may as well be her elderly dog and her books, at least until she goes to college. Rafe is taking community college classes, is in love, and is substance-free except for morning coffee and the occasional psilocybin trip. His growing love of the natural world has inspired him to study microbiology.

These are not happy endings. They are new growth after devastation. Our stories aren't over yet. We keep becoming.

It was the first COVID spring, downy grass embossing the fire-ravaged hills with green for a split second before summer bleached them brown again. Rafe had just graduated, but was robbed of the usual rites of passage. He said he didn't care very much, but Carmen really wanted us to have a prom at home. Feeling grinchy and weary of everything, I gave her a budget of $15 to work some magic. She made comfort-food appetizers, laid fairy lights around the patio, put up a tinsel doorway curtain. The rest of us, infected by her spirit, dressed to the nines: bridesmaids dresses, vintage smoking jackets.

We had a living room graduation ceremony: rising freshman Carmen wore Rafe's cap and walked across the living room to "Pomp and Circumstance" while Peter gravely handed her a certificate.

Then we repurposed a liturgy our church uses for parents and graduating seniors because ritual is such a strong lever for helping us move from one reality to the next. Peter and I each took one of Rafe's hands and looked into his eyes as Carmen read it one line at a time for us to repeat.

> *It has been one of the great joys of my life to get to know you, and watch you grow.*
>
> *I am so glad God gave you to me to teach, protect, love, and launch.*
>
> *Now you are crossing over a threshold into a new adventure.*
>
> *God has been with us all along, and God will go with you into whatever happens next.*

> *May you run and not grow weary*
> *May your heart be filled with song*
> God will go by many names and sometimes no name at all, as
> your faith and doubts continue to assert themselves in new ways. By
> whatever name you know God, may the love of God renew your hope
> even if it seems like hope is lost.
> May this next chapter of our life and your life be filled with
> joy, growth, and challenge in the right proportion to help you keep
> becoming.
> *And may the roads you travel*
> *Always lead you home.*
> *Wherever you go, you will always, always, have a home with us.*

For once, we were all crying at the same time.

Then we went out to our little patio and boogied. Even the straight white guys.

Everyone took turns slow-dancing with everyone else, which is surely a sign that Jesus is still alive and working miracles. We ended with a laughing, whole-bodied family hug, that if I didn't have corroboration, would not believe actually happened.

And then, holding on to each other, we belted out all four minutes and ten seconds of "Don't Stop Believin'" at the top of our lungs.

Chapter 16

DANCE WHEN YOU'RE BROKEN OPEN

Dance, when you're broken open.
Dance, if you've torn the bandage off.
Dance in the middle of the fighting.
Dance in your blood.
Dance when you're perfectly free.
　　　　　—Rumi

Two days before George Floyd died, Mali Watkins was dancing in the streets of my hometown, the island city of Alameda.

Alameda is a place both as close to, and as far as you can get from, the edgy metropolis of Oakland, California, just across a narrow channel in San Francisco Bay. It is tree-lined and peaceful, affectionately called "Mayberry" by some of its residents, with a retro movie theater, an old-fashioned ice cream shop, and ubiquitous 25 MPH signs.

It is also plagued by the kind of ever-present coded, "low-key" racism often seen in once-homogenous suburbs. You can still hear the refrain sung on certain NextDoor channels, the call to "put the bridges up" on Halloween so Black and brown parents can't bring their little Spidermans and princesses over from Oakland to trick or treat in relative safety (and for the full-size Snickers bars).

Mali is a Black man, dapper and dear. He is also on the spectrum. It's part of his spiritual and martial arts practice to dance in the street every day. He describes it as how he gives "wholeness to the world." The neighbors see him and wave. He is a familiar presence, and mostly welcome.

But on this one day in May, someone who didn't know him saw him dancing and called the cops, concern-trolling that he would get hit by a car because he was in the street. Four cop cars showed up. They cuffed him, put him on the ground, kneeled on him, and broke five teeth in the struggle. Neighbors called from the sidelines for the police to stop, but they said, "We can only evaluate his mental health once he is under control."

The arrest spawned huge dance parties by protestors, with every hue of human rocking out in the streets. Over the course of the next month, one Mali became many.

I met Mali at one of those dance parties, and we ended up talking for half an hour. His words were sermonic, brilliant, moving, and fluid, and I don't remember a single one of them. But I knew I was in the presence of someone anointed by God. His deep, liquid eyes poured love on me. I felt baptized by his being.

This, though, I did remember. I told him how gravely sorry I was that he had suffered. His answer surprised me.

"No. No. It all happened just like it was supposed to. It *needed* to happen for everything else to happen." He quoted a line from a song he had written, "There's a method to the madness/There's a special feeling after sadness."

It is dangerous to say that God brings good out of our suffering. Some of us have spent years unbelieving in a God who demands suffering, particularly the suffering of already vulnerable people.

But Mali reminded me that each of us gets to decide for ourselves if our own suffering has a holy purpose. Mali went on to tell me about a piece of the larger purpose that this arc of injustice had brought about.

Every day for months before his arrest, a man had driven by him as he danced. This man was a city employee, and even in his official role and public uniform, he called Mali the N-word.

After Mali's arrest, when the news and video went viral, the man sought him out at a party. He begged his forgiveness. They fell onto each other's necks, weeping. Mali's humanity had never been in question. But his own suffering, made more visible, had unearthed the other man's humanity.

The central question of our lives might be: How much can we heal from the hard things that happen to us? And with it: How do we find meaning and purpose from our woundings? That is a question each one of us needs to answer for ourselves.

When we feel weak, that we are not up to the task of healing and then putting our wounds into the service of others, we do well to remember that God's grace will provide the assist.

Sometimes we can schlepp our way out of trouble, especially if we have someone like Sue, who will shepherd us in our hospital johnnies up and down the long sterile hallways.

Sometimes we can pray our way out.

And sometimes the only thing to do is dance. Even, or especially, when we're broken open.

Cynthia and Phil, colleagues of mine and the founders of InterPlay, a global community dedicated to unlocking the wisdom of the body, call this "exforming." Exforming, says InterPlayer Trish Fairley, is to "shake, laugh, cry, whoop, to get what's inside, out!"

She explains,

> When we watch people receive news that they've won a prize, a competition or learn that they are pregnant they often scream, shake and cry or use a high voice to exclaim the same thing over and over, ("Oh my God, Oh my God, Oh my God!"), often covering their face with their hands. Immediately after I gave birth to our first child I shook uncontrollably, so much so that I couldn't hold the cup of tea that I was given. It slopped everywhere.
>
> Likewise, when one hears of a sudden death of a beloved the body may drop to the floor, start shaking, screaming, or sobbing. In other

words, it knows what to do. It should not be calmed until it's ready to say 'enough' for the moment. After a road accident, people will often shake violently. It's helpful to encourage this and not try to reassure them that everything's okay. When they do feel safe again, after the initial shock, their body will stop exforming.

Dance is one way of taking initiative to exform when the tears won't come, or when they won't stop. When we have something that needs shaking loose or sweating out in high kicks, the wild mosh, the crowd surf.

And dancing together is even better than dancing alone. One Oxford study of pain revealed that dancing in sync with a group made dancers able to bear more pain. (Of course, they didn't control for people who find *any* kind of dancing in public painful.)

Dance is the body's jazz hands for the soul. Dance is God on the move. Dance is what we do when we have too many feelings and not enough words. Dance don't cost a thing, and it belongs to everybody. To dance is to let God move through us, reanimate us no matter what death-dealers are after us, the perichoresis that began before everything, the music of the spheres that will play on long after we are gone.

We dance our babies around the kitchen. We practice TikTok moves in our bedroom for hours. Dance is the mosh pit, the all-night rave, Asian grandmas at Zumba class—all of them just as much church as anything is.

Dance is the seven-year-old Mexican orphan tearing it up on a tile patio the night before Peter and I moved away from Colima; it is every three-year-old in the aisles at church who will not be stopped but just *has* to dance to every hymn.

Dance is the Oakland Ghost Ship, the young ones gathering to rave before fire tore through their bodies, ready to worship at the altar of joy, and now dancing at home with God. It is #BLM protestors breaking curfew in downtown Oakland the week after George Floyd's death, shaking money makers from the tops of cars while police looked on, off-kilter. How do you arrest a dancer?

DANCE WHEN YOU'RE BROKEN OPEN

Dance is every one of you, rising from your own ashes. Every day, someone, somewhere, faces the powers of death. But then they make one little move. They put down the bottle. They call the therapist, the DV hotline, the immigration lawyer. They write their name on the application. If they are lying down, they get up. They join the dance.

To dance is to laugh in the face of death and all its minions. As long as we can dance, they have not won. Whoever "they" are.

Sometimes during the 3 a.m. insomniac stretches I call my alone time with God, I have an echo of the same golden sensation that braced me when I awoke from my near-death dream. It returned at certain moments during chemo.

At the time, I thought it might be the drugs (either the bad ones or the better ones to stop the bad ones), but it has endured. It's a rolling shimmer that always comes without warning, unbidden, when I am alone (not counting the snoring man next to me). My cells explode with joy, as if my soul is trying to climb out of my body, achieving astral projection at last. I try not to breathe, afraid of dislodging the magic, or breaking the string that tethers body to soul.

I imagine it to be a little like what people who have dislocated a shoulder go through: the shoulder remembers that accident and slips out of its socket from time to time. But not only is it painless, it's actually deeply pleasurable. Or rather: it's painful in the sense that too much sensation can be painful, but not frightening. I can't fall asleep after this happens, and take time to linger with happy memories, like the sizzle reel of dance parties from my life.

There were the morning dances with the kids during chemo, three-minute dance parties to Michael Franti in the pumpkin-colored parsonage living room in Somerville to shake off the torpor of sleep or anxiety before school and infusion. A couple summers after chemo ended, my crazy chemo curls grown into a mane of resurrection, I bumped into Franti himself in the VIP box at a Dodgers game thanks to bestie Aisha. "'Say Hey' is one reason I am alive today," I told him.

He gave me tickets and backstage passes to his next show in Boston, where bestie Sue and I jumped up and down like idiots and batted around giant yellow balls during "The Sound of Sunshine," until she put her hip out and my chemo hair was plastered to my sweaty, menopausal face.

There was my Somerville Squad, summer-strong, showing up to be Brave at UCC General Synod, a Broadway ending for my scrappy, sweet church.

And there was First Church Prom the following winter as we said our goodbyes. I look at a photo from that night, five years later, and I feel like I'm looking over God's shoulder from the future. There's Jen and Matthew, both lonelyhearts until I made them come to camp with me as counselors, where they had their first kiss. There's their young son, Henry, and there's Leslie, who they adopted from the Casa. Leslie's now a sophomore at American and has come out as nonbinary. There's Rebecca the Whole Foods chef dancing her ass off, not knowing that eighteen months later her heart would fail in her girlfriend's arms on a Cape Cod beach. There's Jenny, whose Holy-Spirit tears and Bruegger's-Bagels advice to just love Rafe is still bearing fruit. There's a hundred other people I love in that single image, all of them so very alive, either here or beyond the veil, because of how well they love and live. We are reprising our Brave flash mob, each of us with a finger pointing at the sky.

There is my still-new dance partner, First Church Berkeley. I think about the sad dance we did in Berkeley on Election Night 2016, Gloria Gaynor once more belting out to anyone who would listen that we would survive. She was right. Democracy is still in the ICU as I write this, but it's not dead yet.

We circle dance, forty women strong, led by silver-haired Sufi Helen Rubardt at our retreat on the ankles of Mt. Tamalpais, voices and guitar rising up to "You are holy/You are whole, You are always evermore, than we ever understand. You are always at hand."

We are slab dancing in September at Camp Caz high above the Russian River, as our church has done for the last fifty years. We are sweaty and jubilant, toddlers and great-grandmas, getting down to the Electric Slide and Earth Wind & Fire.

DANCE WHEN YOU'RE BROKEN OPEN

And finally, it is Ash Wednesday, 2020. We sit in a circle on the dais as a global pandemic settles its skirts over us. We put ashes on each forehead and say, "From dust you came, to dust you shall return," against the backdrop of news reports sounding an early klaxon of mass death. We hear those words as if for the first time. Whether we live to be old or die too soon, we're all only here for a little while, and what we do with our lives matters.

For the closing anthem, we sing a song by Gungor. In our motley band is Julie, who should have died when hit by a drunk driver but survived seven surgeries to co-parent her two children and now a surprise third. Kara, holding the beat on drums, who was raised in foster care, a dark-skinned woman in a white Midwestern family, never adopted and never accepted, until she found her family in us. On guitar, Michele, who is recovering from time in a psych ward.

Amar, a peacenik seventy-something Sikh, is on piano and flute. He has been known to temporarily break his commitment to nonviolence when it's time to tell white supremacists to fuck the hell off. Dylan, a freshman at Cal, skipped class to come play the cello line.

Together we sing, "You make beautiful things, you make beautiful things out of the dust. You make beautiful things, you make beautiful things out of us."

At the end of worship that night, Ken, a man in his seventies who had long suffered the blues, gives us a benediction. He had recently come back to church after a mystical visitation by the Virgen de Guadalupe gave him new vision. He had become accustomed to a black hole of emptiness at the center of his self, and now instead he saw there the Virgin, offering roses. This vision persisted over the days and months that followed. Grateful, he wanted to share this light.

He invites us to stay seated, or rise up and move, exforming for a liturgical moment of prophetic lamentation for our nation. We roar, we weep, we curse, we cut the air, and we claw the heavens. But then, in the contrariness of God, a shift happens. We accidentally end the moment by fake ballet dancing all over the chancel. All these broken people arise, walk, then dance.

January 2021. I drive to Kaiser Oakland radiology, on the ten-year anniversary of the last day of chemo. There is no Dr. B with the kind eyes and patient bedside manner, no clickety-clack of Nurse Kerry's stilettos on the tile; they are thousands of miles away helping new patients navigate the unthinkable.

Efficient health care workers, masked and plexiglassed against the pandemic, move me through the conveyor belt of care. My oncologist, who has only known me as a healthy person and barely knows me at all, calls me the next day, but I miss it. It is a voicemail she is delighted to leave. "Hi, it's Dr. Yu. Great news—your CT scan shows no evidence of disease! Since it has now been ten years since you completed your treatment, we no longer need to check routine scans. Let me know if you have any questions. Take care!" It is finished.

I smile and saddle up into my running tights for a bad dance-jog, which is exactly what it sounds like. My feet carry me a few blocks behind Oakland Airport to San Francisco Bay. Yesterday's rain has cleared the skies of smoke, and it's all blue as far as I can see, except for a few fog-fingers creeping over the coastal range that separates me from the open Pacific. My eyes, whipped by the wind, pour tears from chemo-scarred lachrymal ducts. My hips protest, janky with osteopenia from chemo-induced menopause. But Lizzo sings strength into my ears, and I do awkward high kicks near a slightly surprised great blue heron and a more supportive audience of three Mexican *abuelos* fishing for their supper.

I still worry about dying, from time to time. I've decided I'm not ready to go. I've had a glimpse of what awaits us on the other side of the Portal, and I know it's Good with a capital G. *And* I'm glad to have a little more time here, on this beautiful plane, with the loves I've already been given, and the loves that still await.

ACKNOWLEDGMENTS

Writing is solitary work, but in a work like this one there is actually a cast of thousands.

First, to my besties: Sue, Sarah, Aisha, Leslie, Ellen, Lupita, and Peter. I am, because you are. Thank you for bringing so much courage, laughter, and wisdom into my life.

Behind those besties, there are so many more besties holding the invisible kite strings that have made my spirit soar, taught me, loved me, and held me through the hardest times. To my Silver Lake siblings Whendi, Val, Anne, Tim, Dan, and so many more; my Supper Club, David, Karla, Goose and Jack and your kids who will someday rule the world; my Book Club/Wine Club/Whine Club sisters Cori, Lisa, Jennifer, and Heather, who are helping me haul ass here in middle age, and a gazillion other friends who continue to bless and fill my life with wisdom, joy, love, and when all else fails, fart jokes.

I honor the beautiful places where I got to escape Pandemic Pandemonium House and write solo, and the people who made them available to me: thank you Pat DeJong and Sam Keen for the most generous offer of your Little House high on a hillside in Sonoma; Lisa Overton for your backyard with yellow lab snuggles and wisteria making a cozy cave.

Thank you to all the architects of my full recovery from cancer: surgeons, oncologists, nurses, personal care assistants, CT techs, receptionists, phlebotomists, and more from Dana Farber Cancer Institute, Brigham and Women's Hospital, and Kaiser Oakland, particularly Dr. James Butrynski, Kerry Beliveau, and Kathleen Polson. To all my chemo drivers, kid-carers, dome-shavers, soup-makers, and every single person who pulled me to the surface when cancer and chemo sucked me to the bottom of a dark lake: thank you.

ACKNOWLEDGMENTS

So much gratitude to the architects of this book itself: to my no-BS straight-talking agent Joy Tutela, my kind and perceptive editor Lil Copan, and all the good folks at Broadleaf Books, and to dear friends who read early drafts and made the book a whole lot better with your sensitivity and wisdom: Melissa Shungu, Sue Donnelly, and Ellen O'Donnell.

Thank you to all the people in all the churches, literal and figurative, who have put up with me over the years. You have helped me grow up as a person and a pastor: Broadview Community Church, Silver Lake Conference Center, First Congregational Branford, Resurrection Lutheran in New Haven, Long Lane School, Casa San Jose, Second Congregational Church, First Church Somerville, and First Church Berkeley UCC. To all the beloveds whose stories I tell here, and to those whose stories didn't make it in—know how much your persistence, curiosity and tenderness in continuing to live through the hardest parts of being human encourage me every day.

I can't name you all, but I want to thank the hundreds of wise pastors I am blessed to know and whose example reminds me constantly why this is still the best gig on the planet.

To all the spiritual directors who have shaped my thinking and helped me feel everything, chief among them: Sister Mary Boretti, Rev. Ken Orth, Rev. Joellynn Monahan, and Rev. Diana Cheifetz.

No acknowledgments would be complete without me naming my earliest best friends: books. When Carmen was suffering from paralyzing loneliness and depression as a result of our move to California, my brother Jesse said, "Read books. Books can be your friends this year, until other kids figure out how cool you are. And books will never betray you."

Some of my favorite books as a child, books that took me to safer places amidst the danger—or at the very least, places with enough good magic amidst the danger when my own world was not, and which made me want to write safe worlds for others: The Chronicles of Narnia, Middle Earth, Mary Poppins, all of Edward Eager, Madeleine L'Engle, Betty Smith, and Isaac Asimov. There are scads of nonfiction authors who have been messing with my head and healing my heart for the last few years, many of them likely already known to you: Richard Rohr, Anne Lamott, Pema Chodron, Cheryl Strayed, Brene Brown, Glennon Doyle, Kate Bowler, Michael Eric Dyson, Rebecca Solnit, Ta-Nehisi Coates, Nadine Burke Harris, Isabelle Wilkerson, Haven Kimmel, and Jenny Odell (and the poet Rumi!). Read Rabbi Abraham Heschel's *The Sabbath* to learn how to let go, and Rabbi Edwin Friedman's *Generation to Generation* to learn how to hold on with healthy boundaries. I continue to read fiction because I'm not a monster, and I'm especially glad for those books with no Hollywood endings, that are all middle and mess, mediocrity and love and loss and more love, just like (hopefully) our real lives.

Speaking of love, loss, and more love: I want to end with a full-body hug for my family. It is not easy having a preacher for a wife/mother/daughter/sister, and I thank you for letting me include your stories in my story. To George/Pa, who in many ways was both mother and father to me. To my stepmom Kathy, who grew up with me. To my mother Susan and stepfather Greg, gone to glory: I hope you have each found a peace and freedom you did not have in this life at your souls' next address. To Sam, Tessa, and Emily: sisters who are also friends. To the jackpot of a family I won through birth and marriage and fostering: Junior, Granny Wendy, Mamgu, Tio Bret and Mary, Tia Carmen and Uncle Brett, Phil and Blythe, Brian, Chris, Auntie Susan, all her kids, and all the glorious cousins!

And especially to Carmen, Rafe (who found us this book's title when *God is Not an Asshole* proved too incendiary) and Peter, my hearth and home. None of us is perfect, or even Good—but we are so good for each other. Thank you for teaching me how to love every day of my life. I'm glad I got to stay.